# DEADLY OBSESSIONS

# DEADLY OBSESSIONS

## Life and death in motor racing

BY

## Phil Shirley

HarperCollins*Publishers*

HarperCollins*Publishers*
77–85 Fulham Palace Road, London W6 8JB
www.fireandwater.com

First published in Great Britain in 2000
by HarperCollins*Publishers*

1 3 5 7 9 10 8 6 4 2

A catalogue record for this book is
available from the British Library.

ISBN 0 00 274030 3

Printed and bound in Great Britain by
Creative Print and Design (Wales), Ebbw Vale

*There are only three sports: bullfighting, motor racing, and mountaineering, all the rest are merely games.*

ERNEST HEMINGWAY


*…Youthful impetuousness and courage are not enough, nor is the will to succeed. To be a driver means that one must be part of the machine for hours, hands at the wheel and gear lever, feet on throttle, clutch, and brake, and eyes on the revolution counter, water, and oil gauge. God help the man who loses control for even a fraction of a second, or who is mastered by emotions and thoughts concerning matters other than racing. The machine will kill him without a doubt…*

RUDOLF CARACCIOLA (MERCEDES), 1901–59

# Contents

# Introduction:

# The Danger Game

*I feel safer in my race car than anywhere else, and that's the God honest truth.*

INDY 500 DRIVER SCOTT BRAYTON,

SHORTLY BEFORE HIS DEATH IN 1996

Motor racing, in any form, is an overwhelming and exciting sport. Whether it's an ultra-sophisticated light-weight Formula One car, hugging the track at well over 200 miles per hour at Silverstone, or a high-powered rally car sliding sideways through the corner of a forest track, the basic premise is the same – a driver, an automobile and a crew of mechanics trying to complete a certain number of laps or kilometres before anybody else does.

But, that's not the only similarity between these two examples of this sport. As frustrating as this is, whether a driver is competing for 'the greatest spectacle in auto racing', the Formula One World Championship, or trying to win a stock car heat race at a local dirt track, there is, and always will be, an element of danger.

It's an element of the sport that was driven home with a vengeance in 1994 as the racing community was shocked by the death of Brazilian Formula One driver Ayrton Senna, who died when he lost control of his car during the San Marino Grand Prix at Imola. Senna had an unshakeable faith in God and in his own ability at the wheel of a racing car. To many he was indestructible and untouchable, and this made his violent death even harder to accept. In many ways it changed motor racing forever.

The death of Senna had a profound effect on me personally. I did not know him as well as others but after several interviews over a three-year period we became friends. The last time we spoke, two months before Imola, he talked about quitting and spending more time with his family. Part of him, his deepest, most spiritual part, wanted out. But he simply ran out of time and the exit door closed with a sickening thud.

As usual, every time a horrific incident occurs, such as Senna's fatal accident, people ask those associated with motor racing, 'How can you be involved with such an unnecessarily dangerous sport?' And they almost always respond with the same answer, which is, 'For the same reason people continue to parachute or hang-glide or play football.'

'How can you compare motor racing and football?' is the usual reply.

Now, granted, you may not see as many deaths in a football game. But the number of injuries may be just as numerous – the only difference being the fashion in which these injuries may occur. In motor racing, injuries come about in a more grotesquely spectacular way.

I have never seen a defender slide into a tackle, at over 190 mph, amidst a cloud of debris, smoke and flames. But I know that there are a large number of broken bones, ripped or torn ligaments, or any number of other injuries, that occur in many of the other 'safer' sports.

The bottom line is this: injuries and deaths can happen anywhere and any time in life.

During the writing of this book I decided to approach several race car drivers to get their feelings on this topic.

I asked Mika Hakkinen, the reigning Formula One World Champion, if hearing of a situation like this affects his personal attitude about racing.

'It doesn't and it can't,' replied Hakkinen, a survivor of more than one big accident in his career. 'A bad crash is simply a part of the sport. You don't hope for it, but it's a reality.'

But don't think that racers simply sit around waiting to be injured. Hakkinen went on to say: 'Knowing that this sport can be a dangerous job is actually good, because it makes you spend more time focusing on safety factors that can help prevent injuries.'

Ferrari driver Michael Schumacher told me that the above-average safety rules that the FIA governing body has implemented brings 'peace of mind to [me]. If you look at the rules, for safety, that we have to meet or exceed,' Schumacher said, 'you'll understand why we feel safe.'

Which leads me to another interesting point that I noticed, while interviewing drivers about this subject. A great majority of these drivers made a point of telling me that, in most instances, they feel much safer while in their race cars than they do while in their street cars.

British American Racing team driver Jacques Villeneuve explained that the 'mutual respect for the other drivers' talents, that have developed over time, helps to quell your fears of a dangerous situation.'

'I don't think there is a driver alive that doesn't think about being hurt,' said Villeneuve, 'but if you let that fear control your actions, then you don't belong in this sport.'

The men beneath the helmets have certainly learned to walk that fine line between high competitive speeds and possible death, not only for the personal satisfaction and the adrenaline rush, but also to put on a great show for the fans.

It is an extreme existence, and the precise opposite of a calm activity. It is a storm of emotion, existing at the extreme rim of man and machine where the danger of death or serious injury makes for great entertainment. So extremes always follow: extremes of good judgement and bad, extremes of right and wrong, extremes of safety and danger, extremes of joy and sorrow, elation and despair, energy and exhaustion, extremes of life and death.

Some ask: Where is the sense? Where is the skill? Where is the art or the beauty? Where is anything except a mindless screeching of tyres and the ceaseless roaring of engines? It has little to do with the Greek ethos of sport as a realization of the power of the human body. Instead the whole motor racing experience promotes the idea of dangerous, reckless driving which is likely to claim a significant number of lives each year, and also every horror that goes with it – speed, power, machismo.

The power of seven hundred horses in a jet-fuelled white-knuckle ride of danger and sometimes death. Insanity? Life at a ridiculous limit? Yes, it is a little crazy, maybe a little bad as well, but motor racing will always be the stuff that dreams are made of, an intoxicating essence of the courage and glory of the human spirit. This natural desire to survive and thrive at the limit of human endurance is the inmost motivation of motor racing. Stripped of fame and fortune, the intentions that underlie the actions of men who drive racing cars are the very fabric of human nature – the reality of pain and pleasure, of death and glory. Here is the art and the beauty. Here is the skill and sense.

Motor racing is about all of these things, and more. It transcends human nature and it is human nature. It is about power and money, death and fear; the ambition to possess power and money is often more to racing drivers than any awareness of the dangers. It is ambition that brings them back to the grid each time. In the words of former British Formula One driver Jonathan Palmer: 'It is a kind of optimism; it is utter confidence in your ability; it is the belief that in the fullness of time you will be appreciated and rewarded; it is the pleasure of doing things to the limit, in putting your ability to the test.'

But death and fear can strangle ambition, squeeze the life out of optimism until it hangs like a corpse from the gallows occupied by those condemned by failure. Because in this deadly game the consequence of failure can be fatal. Men who drive racing cars fear failure, but not half as much as they fear fear itself. Fear is more powerful than power and money and death. Fear fuels motor racing and it impacts upon men more than any other emotion.

Fear of losing, fear of being vulnerable, fear of not being powerful enough, fear of not being in control, fear of not being a real man. And often most powerful of all, fear of being seen as afraid. Male identity is bound up with fear and so is motor racing, even though most racing car drivers won't admit to it. Despite its pervasive presence, fear is an emotion rarely talked about openly by us as men, least of all within the tough, masculine sport of motor racing.

One of the beliefs of traditional masculinity is that a man must not show he is afraid. Riddled with fear he may be, but if he wishes to be seen as a man – a champion and a warrior of men – he must hide his fear behind a mask of fearlessness. A racing car driver hides his face behind a mask of protection and his true emotion behind a mask of bravado. Many drivers are afraid and many drivers pray but few admit to it. It takes a brave man to admit he is afraid or that he prays to ease his fear, especially if failure and fear can mean the difference between life and death.

A few weeks before the start of the 1999 Grand Prix season,

British driver Johnny Herbert said: 'If you're scared, it is a sign of weakness and will affect your possibility of success. But we all get frightened sometimes and we all believe in something even though most of us are not particularly religious.' On the eve of the last Grand Prix season of the twentieth century I asked many of the top Formula One drivers this question: 'Do you ever get frightened and do you believe in God?' Most of them said they believed in God or some supernatural power but hardly any of them admitted to being afraid.

Fear is a dirty word in motor racing. In the words of Jonathan Palmer again: 'We control fear in the same way we control danger. It is minimized until there is scarcely an element of it left.' But still fear lingers. In this book you will hear men who try to control fear use words such as anxiety and dread, apprehension and foreboding. In some cases they are but whispers of conscious thought and other times they are shouts of honesty, confessions as powerful as the very cars that propel them to the edge of sanity.

You will hear racing car drivers open their souls to talk about colleagues who have died; friends, too, who have died on the track. How it makes them angry: angry at the unfairness of it all, angry at the foolishness of it all ... angry at God, maybe. It is a primitive reaction. Motor racing is dangerous because speed is dangerous, and because it is one of the most ferociously competitive sports ever seen. It is harsh and ruthless. There are 22 drivers on the grid at the start of a Grand Prix and the rewards for them are huge; the rewards for those at the front are unbelievable:

The drivers in the leading three positions on the starting grid at Melbourne for the first race of the 1999 Grand Prix season – world champion Mika Hakkinen, David Coulthard and Michael Schumacher – are reputed to be receiving something in the order of £10 million each this year. They, and the rest of the men who drive racing cars for a living, want all the money they can get, not just for its own sake, but because it is the measure of their success. If one driver is getting £10 million a year, then it is everyone's ambition to be a £10 million driver. It shows what you are. It is not the money that brings these men to the track. Money does not make them take impossible risks. But when people get killed, they feel they are worth the money.

Hakkinen explained: 'With 30 per cent of fatal accidents, I think, well, I would have been able to drive out of that one. But with the other 70 per cent, I know I would have had absolutely no chance. Every driver must admit that. And I think of the money and say: well, I deserve this.'

This book is the story of the men who drive racing cars and their place in our lives, and in the pulsating world of power, money and death that is Grand Prix racing; a place where most of us would not survive. These sporting heroes, who risk their lives to pursue a vanishing dream at terrifying speeds, are propelled and possessed by a powerful demon. The demon's name is ambition; a determination to succeed at all costs.

The truth behind the headlines of Grand Prix racing is more sobering than exhilarating, more tragic than triumphant. Beneath the fame, fortune and glamour there is a deep, inextricable layer of truth. When exposed to the light of reality it reveals the fears and hopes of the men whose ambition is more to them than any awareness of the dangers. No amount of money or glamour could disguise the bleakness of this world in which ambition and danger go hand in hand with faith and the fear of death.

This is not a detailed account of the history of Grand Prix racing; you can find that elsewhere. Instead it paints a vivid picture of the spiritual and superstitious side of one of the most ferociously competitive of all sports. And asks how these men with nerves of steel come to terms with living one split second from eternity: by placing their trust not only in natural skill and modern technology, but also in the conviction of the soul and spirit and the existence of a sixth sense.

Essentially, this book is the story of the speed kings who find it impossible to escape from their own mortality in a sport where death is always on the agenda. It is an extreme existence, but the danger of death or serious injury makes for great entertainment. That's a fact of life and a deadly obsession.

Phil Shirley
May 1999

# 1

# The Gates

*They say that if you go to The Gates often enough, eventually they open.*

NIGEL ROEBUCK

For me, the real issue of the sense of motor racing and its place in our lives, hit home with a vengeance in the summer of 1994. It happened a few weeks after the death of Austrian driver Roland Ratzenberger and Brazilian world champion Ayrton Senna, before and during the San Marino Grand Prix at Imola. This was the weekend when, to paraphrase former world champion Niki Lauda, 'God took his hand off Formula One.' It was also a weekend when I and countless other people, fans and participants alike, questioned the sanity of the sport.

On this weekend, midway through the 1994 Grand Prix season, Senna's close friend and fellow Brazilian Rubens Barrichello made a miraculous escape from a smash, Ratzenberger died and so too Senna. And there was more to follow: Monaco came next where Karl Wendlinger suffered severe brain injury, and the year went on with J. J. Lehto and Jean Alesi fracturing their necks and Pedro Lamy breaking his legs.

Ratzenberger was killed during qualifying practice on Saturday 30 April, crashing his Simtek car at colossal speed on the Tosa curve. Senna, who went to the horrifying scene of Ratzenberger's fatal accident, died the following day when the Williams car he was driving hit a concrete wall at the corner called Tamburello at 186 miles per hour.

Both men, for the first time ever in their respective careers, experienced what can only be described as panic attacks shortly before they died; their thoughts, normally calculated, calm and collected, were suddenly thrown into disarray, mingled with sadness and mortality. Ratzenberger, deeply troubled by an accident involving Rubens Barrichello on Friday 29 April at Imola, felt emotional – as though he was on the verge of tears – in the hours leading up to his fatal accident.

The Austrian had never felt this way before, and was both anxious and puzzled by the sudden change. Ominously, his gut feeling was that he should pull out of the San Marino Grand Prix, but he ignored it. Senna, the first to visit Barrichello in the track's medical centre, was deeply affected by Ratzenberger's death, so much so that he telephoned his fiancée, Adrienne Galitseu, and said he did not want to race.

Senna had the same gut feeling as Ratzenberger – that something bad was going to happen – and he also ignored it.

Ratzenberger was so shocked by the unexpected onset of mortality that he did something he'd never done before – he prayed. He didn't really believe in the existence of God and was more interested in putting his faith in human skill and modern technology, but after Barrichello miraculously escaped serious injury and possibly even death when his Sasol-Jordan became airborne and crashed hard at 160 mph, Ratzenberger closed his eyes for a moment and secretly focused on a power greater than himself or the Simtek car that he was about to push to the limits around the Imola track. He didn't really know whom he was talking to but gripped by such an intense feeling of mortality, he found himself praying for a safe qualifying session.

Simtek engineers recall a strangely subdued Ratzenberger on the morning of 30 April 1994. He just couldn't shake the feeling that fate might be conspiring against him, even though he knew the risk factor was the same as always and that his afternoon session on the Imola track would be just like any other qualifying practice.

It wasn't, and in the end, in the sudden, final instant of his life, Roland Ratzenberger could not have known what hit him. He could not have seen what, in the next moment, would kill him. A sudden twist of fate, an eye-blink miscalculation, and then nothing. He lost control of his car and flew off the track to his death at nearly 200 mph. Not even time to regret ignoring his gut feeling.

Ratzenberger's was the first death in Formula One racing in 12 years, and when word reached the paddock, Senna was said to have had the unmistakable look of someone who had just seen his own ghost. For the first time in his career he wanted to quit, there and then, but he couldn't walk away. Senna could not compromise his obsession, and he believed that whatever fate had in store for him out on the track he would react quickly enough to avoid serious injury.

But this was not possible, not even for Senna. When his Williams-Renault FW16 failed to negotiate the sweeping left Tamburello turn, it rocketed off the circuit and into a concrete retaining wall, an impact so instantaneous at a speed approaching 200 mph that he could not have shifted his eyes from the open track ahead in time to see it.

Both Ratzenberger and Senna had seen something – or felt something – on the track that was beyond their ability to comprehend, and it frightened them. In the end it killed them. But they are not the first and won't be the last Grand Prix racing drivers to experience this strange phenomenon.

Seventeen men died and more than one hundred were seriously injured in Grand Prix racing between 1963 and 1997. These were the speed kings who tried and failed to escape their own mortality. Among the fatalities are three other men who, like Ratzenberger and Senna, experienced the sudden onset of an overwhelming feeling of the fragility of flesh and blood shortly before dying on the track.

Ronnie Peterson, Gilles Villeneuve and Ricardo Paletti were suddenly gripped by the awful realization that their luck was about to run out. It was the same deep, nagging anxiety that accompanied Ratzenberger and Senna to their respective awful deaths. Maybe these four men, all highly intelligent and extraordinarily skilful Grand Prix drivers, were so in touch with their innermost being, or so tuned in to some kind of sixth sense, that they received a transcendent warning to quit.

But because Grand Prix drivers are largely men of iron nerve and will, and possess sharp intellect, senses beyond human grasp, belief or reasoning are almost always dismissed, or at the very least psychologically dissected. Formula One is as much about mental energy as physical energy. It is not simply about men racing each other to see who is the most skilful or whose car is faster. There is another level of competition, a contest between men's minds, and also a level above that: a contest between a man's own mind and his own mortality.

Ronnie Peterson died in September 1978 after the Lotus car he was driving crashed during the Italian Grand Prix at Monza. A few hours before the end of his life the Swedish driver became deeply troubled. He had had a bad weekend with a series of misfortunes to his car, but it was more than that which bothered him during his final hours.

On the outside he appeared happy and relaxed, joking with his Lotus team-mate Mario Andretti, but inside Peterson felt anxious, afraid even. He had telephoned his wife to say that he didn't want to race. He couldn't explain why, but something was wrong. Unlike Senna, Peterson was not a religious or superstitious man, and that is probably why he dismissed the thing that troubled him before the 1978 Italian Grand Prix as a combination of tiredness and stress.

What happened within seconds of the start was described by *Motorsport* (October 1978) as follows:

*Patrese was on the right-hand side of the pack trying to overtake Hunt, as they funnelled into the road circuit, and the Arrows hit the McLaren, which bounced across the road into Peterson's Lotus which in turn was spun across the road into the right-hand guard rail and was struck by Brambilla's Surtees that was trying to avoid the melee down the right-hand side.*

James Hunt, the Englishman who won the 1976 world title and who sadly died in June 1993, pulled Peterson out of the car and out of the flames. Ironically, before the race, Hunt commented to a Lotus engineer that 'Ronnie doesn't look himself today.' Hunt kept thinking about that as he walked back to the pits while Peterson, his yellow overalls stained with blood and oil, lay on the track a few yards away from the remains of his black Lotus.

He was conscious and rational but both his legs were badly smashed, and he had burns on the shoulder and chest. X-rays revealed more than 25 fractures in both legs and feet. Following surgery, Peterson developed breathing difficulties. He had developed multiple emboli (small obstructions due to blood clots or fat globules) in his lungs. His kidney function had also declined, and urinary output had deteriorated. He was unconscious and neurological examination showed that he had signs of severe brain damage.

The autopsy confirmed fat embolism as the cause of Ronnie Peterson's death; fat globules were evident in the lungs, kidneys and brain.

His death was a great tragedy for Formula One, especially because he had been offered a number one position with McLaren. After racing as Lotus number two to Mario Andretti, Peterson was about to get his big chance, almost nine years after making his Formula One debut in 1970.

That was with the March team, the same team he had been racing for in the junior formula. He immediately impressed the world with his raw speed. In 1971 he scored five second-place finishes and was runner-up to Jackie Stewart in the world championship, but it was not until he left for Lotus in 1973 that he won his first race, at the French Grand Prix. Teaming with Emerson Fittipaldi, the current world champion, he was proving to be more than a match for the Brazilian. He went on to win three more races that year and finished third in the world championship. Fittipaldi soon left for McLaren and Ronnie Peterson continued with Lotus as the team leader for the next two years.

After an unproductive return to March in 1976 to drive the six-wheel Tyrrell, Peterson returned to Lotus as a number two to Mario Andretti in 1978. Together they dominated the 1978 season in the Lotus 79 with Peterson scoring a pair of spectacular wins. He even outqualified his team-mate at Brands Hatch even though he was using hard compound tyres, rather than the usual and more suitable tyres used for qualifying sessions, and had only a half tank of gas. After his victory at Zeltweg in Austria he trailed Andretti by only nine points with four races remaining. It was well known that he would be with another team in 1979 and some suggested that he should just go for the championship with nothing to lose.

But Peterson was a man of his word: 'I'm going to McLaren next year,' he said. 'It's not announced yet, but Mario knows, some of these people,' he sighed, 'who say I should forget our agreement now ... I don't understand them. I had open eyes when I signed the contract, and I also gave my word. If I break it now, who will ever trust me again?'

Maybe Peterson should have trusted his own instinct more. On that fateful afternoon at Monza something told him to walk away from the Italian Grand Prix. The same thing that caused Ratzenberger and Senna to fear the worst at Imola 16 years later. Now the image of Peterson racing through the most dangerous curves, absolutely on the limit with tyres squealing and using just enough opposite lock and throttle to control his car, is darkened by the memory of Monza, 1978.

'I remember seeing Ronnie walking to the Lotus motorhome shortly before the race,' Hunt recalled some years later. 'He had the look of a man who was worried about something, and that was out of character for Ronnie. He was a happy-go-lucky guy, a great driver, and a genuine character that loved his job and was very good at it. I said, "Hey Ronnie, everything okay?" He turned and smiled and gave me the thumbs up, so I thought I must have been mistaken. Now I'm not so sure. Maybe something was bothering him.'

Gilles Villeneuve certainly had something on his mind on the morning of Saturday 8 May 1982, and it wasn't only revenge. The French-Canadian driver brooded and sulked as he plotted to get even with his Ferrari team-mate Didier Pironi during qualifying for the Belgian Grand Prix at Zolder, but as he burned with the thought of retribution, a different, more threatening, deep gloom descended on Villeneuve.

At first he could not identify the nature of the depression, but as the hours ticked slowly by and it was almost time for him to take his Ferrari out on the Zolder track, Villeneuve suddenly realized what was wrong. He was not only consumed by a thirst for revenge, he was afraid as well. Deeply conscious of his own mortality and, for the first time in his life, frightened of death, he was being haunted by the demons of his own ambition. Like Ayrton Senna, Gilles Villeneuve had seen his own shadow, only it was faded and ghostly.

A still, small voice inside Villeneuve said: 'Don't race today. There is danger out there. Death stalks Zolder ... looking for you Gilles, waiting for you.'

Joseph Gilles Henri Villeneuve, born 18 January 1950, always drove to the limit. He was perhaps born for speed, destined to court danger. Niki Lauda wrote of him, 'He was the craziest devil I ever came across in Formula 1 ... The fact that, for all this, he was a sensitive and loveable character rather than an out-and-out hell-raiser made him such a unique human being.' Flying, snowmobiling or driving – even with his wife Joann, he was a risk-taker of classic proportions. Yet his fellow drivers said that on the track he was scrupulously fair and did not put anyone's safety other than his own in jeopardy.

Villeneuve's biggest mistake, perhaps, was to believe in his own immortality, or invincibility behind the wheel, but strangely other people believed it as well. It was as though his supreme confidence as a driver, or pilot, of exceptional ability and unparalleled judgement, just rubbed off and sank in whoever was unlucky enough to ride with him. Villeneuve would scare you to death, but he'd get you there in one piece, and quickly.

Professor Sid Watkins, Formula One's permanent chief medical officer, in his book *Life at the Limit* (Pan, 1997), wrote of Villeneuve that he

> *once had the misfortune to meet him in the lobby of the hotel at Sao Paulo, where he offered me a lift to Interlagos. Madame Villeneuve was with him so when we got to his rented car, I moved to sit in the rear, but Madame insisted that I sat in the front. Gilles in a road car was frightening and when I turned to speak to his wife she was not visible, as she had taken to the floor. She indicated that this was normal for her and I soon found out why.*
>
> *Villeneuve believed in the 'gap theory' – i.e. that there was always a space into which he could move when faced with a high-speed collision. He ignored all the red lights, gently bounced off parked cars or lampposts, talking all the time and never pausing or hesitating in the traffic. On getting to the circuit, he asked if I wanted a lift back later!*

Villeneuve adhered to the same 'gap theory' in all situations. It showed little consideration for his passengers or other road users and, despite Villeneuve's undisputed skill as a driver, it was largely subject to the law of chance. He relied on luck and other people getting out of the way in time and in the right direction. It was this combination that conspired against him at Zolder on 8 May 1982.

According to Watkins, Villeneuve was living on borrowed time. Had Formula One not killed him, a road accident or helicopter crash would have. Villeneuve, when all is said and done, was a loose cannon. His methods used in flying helicopters were irresponsible and outrageous. He frequently took off with the fuel gauge at zero, flying in and out of power cables and pylons without a care in the world. To many Villeneuve's death, when it came, was no surprise. To some, though, it was a surprise that it had not come earlier, much earlier.

Gilles Villeneuve rose up through snowmobile racing in Quebec. These dangerous machines were the first vehicles he raced and the first to put his life at risk. He said: 'Every winter, you would reckon the ice at 100 mph. Those things used to slide a lot, which taught me a great deal about control. And the visibility was terrible! Unless you were leading, you could see nothing, with all the snow blowing about. Good for the reactions.'

His first Formula One race was at Silverstone in 1977 partnering James Hunt and Jochen Mass, the German driver involved in Villeneuve's fatal crash five years later. Towards the end of the '77 season Villeneuve had established a reputation as a promising talent, although McLaren team boss Teddy Mayer, due partly to Marlboro sponsorship considerations, declined to keep Villeneuve, momentarily leaving the promising young driver high and dry for the following season until Ferrari came knocking. It was a dream come true for Villeneuve who would later remark: 'If someone said to me that you can have three wishes, my first would have been to get into racing, my second to be in Formula One, my third to drive for Ferrari ...'

The French-Canadian's Ferrari career, however, began in a less than auspicious fashion. In the Mosport race he left the course on someone else's oil. The next race, at Fuji, saw him leave the track again, but this time at the cost of some spectators' lives. Villeneuve was deeply upset, but his propensity for risk-taking was unabated, and his love for the sport was as pure as the adrenaline that surged through him every time he raced.

Former world champion Keke Rosberg, with whom Villeneuve had many a joust on the track, said of him: 'In a race car, he was the hardest bastard I ever knew, but absolutely fair.'

Nigel Roebuck, *Autosport*'s Grand Prix editor who became a good friend of Gilles Villeneuve, felt that he was 'the fastest racing driver in the history of the sport', a description applied to him first by his former Ferrari team-mate Jody Scheckter. 'There may have been greater, certainly in terms of success, but none with more freakish car control,' concluded Roebuck.

By the end of the seventies, Villeneuve's all-or-nothing approach was well known, and it was the manner in which he raced rather than the outcome of his races that inspired the most. It is no surprise, therefore, that his signature race was not a first, but a second. At the 1979 French Grand Prix at Dijon, Renault and Jean-Pierre Jabouille posted the first win for a modern turbo car. According to the Grand Prix Hall of Fame:

*Rene Arnoux, running well, looked to make it a Renault one-two. Villeneuve, however, asserted a definite* au contraire *in a sliding, wheel-banging, tire-boiling duel with Arnoux that no witness to it is likely to forget. Villeneuve's insane insistence that his slower Ferrari could beat Arnoux's faster Renault was rewarded, and he finished just ahead of the Frenchman. It is probably safe to say that this was the most exciting race for second place in the history of motor racing.*

Another example of Villeneuve's 'insane' determination was at Watkins Glen in 1979, during first qualifying for the United States Grand Prix. Villeneuve had been 11 seconds faster than anyone else in the downpour which engulfed the circuit and his Ferrari T4. His team-mate Jody Scheckter was second fastest. One of Villeneuve's rivals, Jacques Laffite, said: 'He's not like the rest of us, he's on a separate level. He has no fear.'

In his biography of the driver, Roebuck reported on a conversation with him when Villeneuve made clear his lack of fear of accidents. 'I don't have any fear of a crash,' he said. 'OK, on a fifth-gear corner I don't want to crash – I'm not crazy. If I feel I'm going to put a wheel on the grass, I'm going to lift a bit, like anyone else. But if it's near the end of qualifying, and you are trying for pole position maybe, then I guess you can squeeze the fear.'

At Monte Carlo in 1978 Villeneuve narrowly escaped serious injury after crashing during the Monaco Grand Prix. It was a bad accident and Villeneuve was lucky to walk away, but when interviewed after the race he claimed: 'I was not frightened at all. My only fear was for the car. I thought, "Bloody hell, I'm going to have a nice one here." But you know you just go like this ...' Villeneuve then stuck out his arms, screwed up his face and pretended to brace for an impact as if it was all a big joke.

But he was being sincere. Gilles Villeneuve genuinely had no fear of accidents, fatal or otherwise, and in his heart and mind there was no such thing as one risk too many. He always raced to the limit of human and mechanical endurance. He always took chances.

On Saturday 8 May 1982 at Zolder, a pine forest-framed racing track in the Flemish corner of Belgium, Villeneuve was taking more chances, only now the difference was that he had no peace of mind. The usual calm, calculated and also happy-go-lucky Villeneuve was all screwed up on the inside. His every action and thought was affected by the deep gloom caused by his bitter rivalry with Ferrari team-mate Didier Pironi and the strange anxious churning of his heart and mind; the turning of his own mortality beneath the hard exterior that earned him Keke Rosberg's title 'the hardest bastard I ever knew'.

It didn't help that for the previous 12 days Villeneuve's mind had been in turmoil at Pironi's audacious and wounding victory at the previous race, the San Marino Grand Prix at Imola. Villeneuve despised Pironi for failing to honour an unspoken code at Imola, where he won, in Villeneuve's opinion, improperly. But now, at Zolder, Villeneuve's burning quest for revenge was also mingled with fear. For the first time in his career, the French-Canadian was frightened of having an accident. He didn't know why and, as Pironi would later reveal, 'He would not even admit it to himself. But something more than our rivalry was eating away inside him. Maybe he suddenly realized that he was human after all.'

What exactly was going through Villeneuve's mind as he hurtled around Zolder at breathtaking speeds in a desperate bid to overhaul Pironi's best qualifying lap, will never be known. It went with Villeneuve to his grave. But as the final minutes of his life flew by, one thing must have been clear to Villeneuve: as hard as he tried, he was not going to beat Pironi's time. The Ferrari team knew this and put out a signal to come in at the end of the next lap. Villeneuve did not respond and he did not come back.

As Timothy Collings describes in his book *The New Villeneuve* (Bloomsbury, 1997):

*Halfway round his lap, he [Gilles Villeneuve] went through the chicane and sped up and over the hill which followed towards the next corner, to the left, and its successor, to the right. In the distance, he could see a slow car which he knew, by instinct, would be on his best line at the corner to the right; and so the question was: to brake or to power on, foot down on the throttle, and find the gap on one side or the other. For this man there was no need to reflect or think. He always drove to the limit.*

*He kept his foot down. Flat. The car ahead was a March, driven by Jochen Mass of Germany. Mass was coasting back towards the pits, having given his all in his qualifying run to secure his place in what was scheduled to be his 100th Grand Prix. Mass noticed a flash of red in his mirror and opted to keep to the right, a move designed to allow Villeneuve to pass on the left and have a better and more usual line for the turn. The French-Canadian, however, had decided that this would not happen and that a gap would materialize to the right, not the left, of Mass's car. He had selected to attack a non-existent space towards the right of the track and had not given himself any room, or time, for error. The left front tyre of his Ferrari touched the rear right tyre of the March and, quite literally, took off.*

The Ferrari of Gilles Villeneuve was airborne for what seemed like an eternity, but in truth was only a matter of seconds, before nose-diving with great energy and sickening force and somersaulting across the track.

The front of the Ferrari snapped away, Villeneuve's helmet was pulled off and the driver hurled, like a rag doll, into the wire-mesh catch fencing at the side of the track, on the outside of the corner. Villeneuve was still wrapped in his seatbelts, which were connected to a lump of sheet metal torn out of the chassis.

He was not breathing and had suffered a fatal fracture of the neck just where the spine meets the base of the skull.

# 2

# Fatal Attraction

*I don't have any fear of a crash. No fear of that. Of course, on a fifth gear corner with a fence outside, I don't want to crash. I'm not crazy. But if it's near the end of practice, and you're trying for pole position maybe, I guess you can squeeze the fear ...*

GILLES VILLENEUVE

Villeneuve's bloody and horrific death left a dark stain on Formula One and overshadowed the career and life of Jochen Mass. The German suffered with the memory of the Zolder accident and its after-effects for many years. 'I remain haunted by it,' he admitted. 'In the end it made me stop racing, even though I know I did nothing wrong.

'It made me question my own mortality, because when you live life at the limit sooner or later you must face up to the possibility of serious injury or death. One day I woke up and looked at my wife and children and thought, "Enough is enough, no more risks".'

Nigel Roebuck added: 'I always doubted Gilles Villeneuve would survive this sport. Formula One was infinitely more perilous then than now, and they say that if you go to The Gates often enough, eventually they open. Gilles, always at the bitter limit, and frequently over it, would take one chance too many, which ultimately he did.'

Villeneuve didn't believe in the myth about 'The Gates', instead he accepted the risks involved with his own kind of fatalism. Before his first victory in Formula One at the 1978 Canadian Grand Prix at the Ile de Notre-Dame circuit in Montreal – later to be renamed after him – Villeneuve was cross-examined by a Quebec newspaper about whether Formula One was more dangerous than snowmobile racing. 'Which is more likely to kill you?' he was asked. 'None,' came the reply, 'I'm more afraid of dying of old age.'

He need not have worried. Villeneuve was only 32 when he died on the track at Zolder, and James Hunt said: 'Gilles loved life and I am sure that had he survived the accident without serious injury he would have continued to push himself and his car to the limit. That's the kind of guy he was, a daredevil. He loved danger, but maybe he did sense something was wrong.

'Maybe he felt that fate was turning against him. Maybe Ronnie Peterson experienced the same thing before his accident at Monza. I'm not sure what they were thinking, but I am sure that this feeling of mortality, when you question the sense of it all, happens to us all. There were one or two occasions during my racing career, following bad accidents, when I felt down – but for me the risk of serious injury or death came with the territory – but you rarely gave it a second thought because as a professional racing car driver you do everything in your power to control your fate, or destiny. Instinct plays a part, but emotion ... well, that's unreliable, dangerous!'

Villeneuve's Ferrari team-mate Didier Pironi and rival driver Ricardo Paletti were very emotional on the day of the Canadian Grand Prix at Ile de Notre-Dame in June 1982, less than two months after Villeneuve's death at Zolder. Pironi, who had carried Villeneuve's helmet back from the scene of his fatal accident to the Ferrari motorhome, could not shake off the heavy sense of foreboding that remained around him. He had suffered nightmares and had a vague feeling of dread during the build-up to the Canadian race. Paletti was also troubled. Normally cool and easy-going, he felt uptight and, like Pironi, could not shake off a sense of dread about the race he was about to take part in.

At the start, Pironi's Ferrari stalled. The following cars had to drive either side of his stationary vehicle, but one from the back, driven by Paletti, crashed into him at 125 mph. It was a huge collision and it was followed by flames. Chief Medical Officer Professor Sid Watkins recalled: 'There was a massive impact and both cars were hurled down the circuit. Paletti's car went to the right and the Ferrari of Pironi down the circuit to the left. As we passed Pironi I could see he was all right and struggling out of the car. Paletti, however, was slumped in the cockpit.

'I opened Paletti's visor. He was deeply unconscious, so I thrust an airway into his mouth and lifted his eyelids to inspect his pupils.

They were dilated. I had heard consciously, but as at a distance, the sound of running fluid, which I realized was fuel. At that moment there was a whoosh of an explosive burst of flame, which shot high in the air. The legs of my uniform had absorbed fuel and ignited. I'd closed Paletti's visor to protect him as the fire fighters arrived. It was all a matter of seconds between the accident and the fire – I reached Paletti 16 seconds after the impact.'

But Paletti was already dying. The fire was quickly put out and the young driver, who had had the steering wheel and column jammed in his chest during impact, eventually released from the wreckage. He went straight to hospital where, shortly after arrival, he was pronounced to have lost his life from massive chest and abdominal injuries. Several months later the truth came out. Paletti's mother, who had been at trackside to witness the horrific accident, revealed: 'The death of Gilles Villeneuve had frightened Ricardo. I told him not to race at Montreal, but he didn't want to let the team down. I wished he had listened to me.'

And Pironi wished he had listened to his own heart. After being close to two fatal accidents within two months – Villeneuve at Zolder and Paletti at Ile de Notre-Dame – the Frenchman was visibly shaken and, more significantly, deeply troubled. Close friends and family told him to take some time off. They sensed that Pironi was experiencing some kind of inner turmoil. He had seen his team-mate Villeneuve killed horribly and stood by the side of Paletti's burning car as the young driver's life expired while the flames were extinguished.

A few days before the German Grand Prix at Hockenheim, only a few weeks after the tragedy of Ile de Notre-Dame, Pironi had a terrible nightmare. In it, he stood rooted to the spot, unable to move, as Villeneuve's Ferrari dropped out of the sky and crushed him. As he lay on the track, dying, Villeneuve, his face a mask of blood, stood over him. Pironi was staring up at Villeneuve's ghost. It was also raining, heavily.

On the day of the 1982 German Grand Prix, Pironi said a quiet prayer before getting into his Ferrari. He was in pole position and in the lead for the world championship. It had been raining and the wet conditions at Hockenheim concerned him. He could not see through the spray and crashed into the back of fellow Frenchman Alain Prost's Renault. The effect was an accident that mirrored Villeneuve's at Zolder: the Ferrari flew up and away, somersaulting for a few seconds, before crashing hard further down the track. The impact was massive. Pironi shattered both legs, but he was alive.

The accident ended his career as a Formula One driver but his thirst for speed remained unquenched and he took up powerboat racing. Two years after his accident at Hockenheim, Pironi admitted: 'I think someone up there was telling me something ... get out of racing. First Gilles, then Paletti. After Hockenheim I said to myself, "Didier, enough is enough. Quit while you are still alive." I miss Formula One but at least I can enjoy the rest of my life.'

Unfortunately, Pironi died in a powerboat racing accident in August 1987. He was racing in the Needles Trophy off the Isle of Wight when his boat flipped at 100 mph as it crossed the wake of a tanker. A few months later, his girlfriend gave birth to twin boys and named them Didier – and Gilles. They inherited the memory of a father who could not quit.

In the end Didier Pironi went to 'The Gates' in a powerboat and they opened for him. Maybe all of them, Pironi, Paletti, Ratzenberger, Senna and Villeneuve, went to 'The Gates' once too often; took one risk too many; dismissed the heavy sense of fore-boding as just stress or tiredness, or emotion. Maybe they were given a chance to walk away while they still had the chance, maybe not. Perhaps it was impossible for them not to race. I believe so.

Ratzenberger searched his soul after Rubens Barrichello came close to death but his fear was not enough to keep him away from the track; Senna saw his own shadow in the darkening of the sport in the wake of Ratzenberger's death but still chose to continue racing; Villeneuve suddenly realized his own mortality and took more risks than usual to bully the feeling of vulnerability into submission; Paletti and Pironi wanted to get out but were held fast by ambition, pride even.

In the end the deadly obsession with speed killed each of them. They went out in a blaze of glory, doing what they loved best. Racing. Only one of them, Ayrton Senna, doubted his calling – but more of that later. The truth is, Formula One is powerfully addic-tive; a drug impossible to kick, especially if you happen to be a racing driver. They are perhaps the luckiest men alive, when they are still lucky and still alive and winning. The fame and fortune. Oh boy, it's a road paved with gold. Blood and guts sometimes, yes, but more often than not all the riches a man can hold, and more.

Adulation and exhilaration. 'It's better than sex,' Pironi once remarked. But sometimes the things we love the most kill us in the end. Speed thrills and the love of speed kills. If there is a spiritual thread through the lives of the men you have just read about, and some will dispute the existence of such a supernatural undercurrent, it may never be properly understood. In truth, it is perhaps too unprovable, too prone to suggestions of fate, and too sinister. But, even in the cold light of reality, it cannot be ignored.

Listen to Patrick Tambay's chilling story. The unemotional, often cold-hearted Ferrari driver, hired to replace Gilles Villeneuve in his car, number 27, had a supernatural encounter during the 1983 San Marino Grand Prix at Imola, a year after Didier Pironi's victory at the same track. Then Villeneuve had started third and later accused his team-mate Pironi of winning improperly. The 'bad blood' between them played a part in Villeneuve's death during qualifying for the 1982 Belgian Grand Prix when he crashed trying to beat Pironi's lap time.

Less than a year after Villeneuve's death, Patrick Tambay arrived at his place before the start of the San Marino Grand Prix and found an unexpected message: it was painted on the track, at position number three – a Canadian maple leaf flag and under it was written 'Win for Gilles'. Tambay was so moved he wept.

The race itself was a breathtaking duel between Tambay's chasing Ferrari and the Brabham of Italy's Riccardo Patrese. Tambay passed him and won, but afterwards was strangely subdued. He felt somehow removed from one of the greatest moments of his life, as though he was there in body but not in spirit. Tambay had the look of a man who had seen a ghost.

Much later he admitted: 'Something strange happened to me during that race. I was not alone in the car that day. Gilles was with me; I had been talking to him through the whole race. He had been robbed the year before and could not rest in peace. But he was in peace now.'

Perhaps, when you live close to the edge, the line between life and death is so thin that eventually it fades into nothing, the natural and supernatural mingle and entangle until they become insepa-rable, especially during the intensity of a two-hour Formula One race. Pironi once admitted: 'Sometimes, I frighten myself, because all of a sudden I realize I have been operating on some kind of autopilot. I can't remember the last few laps and I wonder where have I been for the past ten minutes or so. My heart, mind, body and car fused into one force. An out-of-body experience, of sorts.'

And Ayrton Senna, during practice at Monaco, when he beat the lap record six times in a row, also experienced an out-of-body sensation. Patrick Fauré, the then Renault Sport manager, said: 'At one point Ayrton braked because he suddenly realized that he was pushing the car far beyond his own ability. He felt detached from his body and was hovering above it all.'

'It is pure intensity,' Senna remarked. 'In the blink of an eye we race close to the point where life meets death. What we do is violent and beautiful, savage and yet so refined. So mortal but living life to the full. This sport can break the body, crush the soul, but make the spirit soar.'

## 3

# Ferocity and Velocity

*The speed with which we wear out our clothes only emphasizes what a violent sport Formula One is.*

OLIVIER PANIS

To understand fully the emotional problems of competing in the world's most dangerous sport, you have to appreciate just what it's like to race a Formula One car. The physical and mental strain is enough to seriously damage an average person; in fact most people would just cave in under the pressure. Little wonder, then, that many, many drivers find it difficult to adjust to normal living after being subjected to the rigours of Grand Prix racing. To survive and thrive in this insane world of danger, power and speed you have to become part man, part machine. And, more significantly, you have to become detached, or immune, from emotion, at least for the duration of a race. 'Man and machine become one,' Senna once remarked. 'Every fibre, every measurement of energy and power, every thought and calculation, every movement, become one.

'Together, man and machine, performing at the limit, and sometimes beyond the limit, of their respective abilities, are able to achieve the impossible.' Not that Senna was, or any other driver is, any kind of automaton or robot, but the fallacy that one can just get into a Grand Prix car and go racing is completely false. Yet it is often believed by those who do not follow the sport with much interest. As Professor Sid Watkins explains in his book *Life At The Limit*:

*Driving a vibrating Formula One car, with virtually no suspension, under the emotional pressures experienced by the drivers, working physically at high ambient and body temperatures, threatened by dehydration and sustaining G-forces which increase their body weight by a factor of 4 truly represents the limits of human performance and sometimes tolerance – apart from the dangers of death or injury if a serious error of judgement or mechanical failure occurs.*

Human error and mechanical failure occur frequently, and irrespective of how well man and machine combine. Senna more than once experienced the feeling of being detached from his body while driving, of operating on some kind of autopilot, so fused, mentally and physically, with the machine that, for a short time, he forgot he was actually driving the car. But emotion would always, at some point, override this robotic state and Senna would suddenly brake. It was like a mild sense of panic – the sudden awareness of mortality perhaps, and the realization that you can only push the limits of ability, both human and mechanical, so far before a serious error of judgement or mechanical failure occurs.

Motor sport safety has come an enormous distance in a relatively short time. The last 30 years have seen major changes to the vehicles, the drivers, the circuits and the response to an incident. While the initial problem with making cars safe was money, now it is an assumed expense for a race team. Thirty years ago, death was an accepted part of the game, these days it is an exception. Many of the newest developments are in safety, especially now that so much computerized technology has been banned from the sport.

In Formula One, there is a huge set of regulations relating to vehicle design. While aerodynamics is virtually free, the dimensions and strength of the cars are strictly enforced. The drivers must be contained within a 'safety cell' in the car. This safety cell must allow the drivers to exit the vehicle and replace the steering wheel within 10 seconds, from a fully seated and strapped-in position. The cross-sections of all openings are controlled, as are minimum widths of the materials permitted. The safety cells must undergo extensive load testing, which is described in detail in Appendix 3 of the FIA technical regulations. All safety cells produced must be tested, one of each new design to destruction. A substantial amount of padding is required around the driver, especially around the head region, to protect the driver as his head is thrown around.

In front of the safety cell, but firmly attached, there must be an energy-absorbing structure that must also pass various tests.

Likewise, on the sides of the safety cell, there must also be energy-absorbing structures. In Formula One, these house the water and oil radiators. The driver's feet must not sit forward of the centre line of the front wheels. Roll-over structures must be in place both behind and in front of the driver, with a line drawn from the top of each clearing the driver's helmet by at least 50mm.

An automatic fire extinguishing system must be fitted, capable of being manually triggered either by the driver or from outside the vehicle by emergency personnel. Data recorders, the fire extinguishing system and the fuel cells must also be contained within the driver's safety cell. The driver must be able to isolate the vehicle's electrical system from the normal seating position. The wheels and tyres of all Formula One cars must have safety hubs fitted to retain the wheel in the event of it coming loose. Brakes must be of standard type and material. The fuel used must be identical for all cars and must burn with a visible flame. Fuel filling procedures must ensure maximum safety and minimum risk to all people in the pit area. All the pit crew are protected by fire-resistant clothing similar to the driver's in the event of a refuelling fire.

Drivers in all forms of motor sport wear protective clothing. The standard overalls are made from Nomex for fire protection. Helmets are compulsory in all forms of motor sport almost wherever racing is found. Gloves and boots are also fire-resistant to ensure all-over protection. In Formula One, new straps have been introduced which attach the helmet to the overalls at the back of the driver's head. These straps prevent the neck being extended during a forward impact. They were a reaction to Mika Hakkinen's accident in Adelaide in 1995 where Hakkinen's neck extended by 120mm upon impact. There are straps on the shoulders of racing overalls that are used as handles for extracting the driver from a damaged vehicle.

The drivers may have lost many of their suicidal tendencies, but the level of safety has brought in some undesirable attitudes towards racing. This is due to the tracks and cars becoming so safe that if a driver does push too hard, he knows that he has a very good chance of walking away with no injuries. There are no consequences for drivers any more. They are paid to drive – if they damage a car, they do not have to pay for it themselves, so why should they care?

Some people believe that if racing safety continues the way it is going the sport may well start to see a decline in revenue as people turn away from it due to boredom. People don't watch motor sport to just see cars following each other around a circuit; they watch it for action. Seeing cars fighting for position, making bold overtaking moves and a few accidents is what it is all about. The drivers don't race because it is safe, they race because of the danger, even though quite often they appear oblivious – or immune – to the risks involved.

Senna was often criticized for being more of a machine than a man, and when, in 1997, Canadian baseball player Larry Walker hit out at Jacques Villeneuve after being beaten into second place as 'Canadian Male Athlete of the Year', by saying that he 'was beaten by a machine and not a man', there was indeed a faint ring of truth to the insult. In this case the machine was the man. The truth is, the top drivers have to be as well tuned and durable as the cars they race.

To be able to push a car at speeds of up to 200 mph round a circuit with maybe 20-odd corners, suffering multiple G-force stress to the neck and shoulders at each turn, for up to two hours at a stretch can only be achieved with a constant attention to one's physical capabilities. Clearheadedness, lightning-fast reactions in an environment with a temperature often on the wrong side of 40°C, being able to hold a conversation via the radio to the pits and be mindful of signals, warning flags and traffic approaching at speed from behind is not the easiest way to become a successful sportsman. 'We work hard, we sweat hard,' Villeneuve has said. 'We're in the car for two hours on race day. There's a lot of endurance necessary.'

The demands that today's highly developed machinery puts on drivers make it impossible to compete without being in peak physical condition. The days of the cigarette-puffing driver holding aloft his winning trophy or downing a glass or two of champagne before the start of a race are over. The current crop of drivers are as much athletes as any Olympic gold medallist and will devote several hours each day to their physical training and mental preparation. Their lives depend on it, in more ways than one.

The revealing report *Evaluation and Perspectives of Medical Study on Race Car Drivers* by J.P. Richalet and C. Bertrand, published in 1983, showed that 'Drivers' pulse rates while racing peak at levels close to the point of human tolerance'. In practice in Monaco, Ferrari driver Didier Pironi's pulse rate peaked at 212 per minute and Gilles Villeneuve's cardiac responses while making intense effort at the end of the practice session for the French Grand Prix reached a maximum of 182. Drivers attained similar cardiac rates during the 1997 and

1998 Grand Prix season – the result of demands placed on the heart by factors such as emotional stress, fear, anger, pressure to excel, raised body temperature, G-forces and muscular effort.

Being fit, therefore, is essential to sustain these cardiac effects and drivers exercise heavily to build up muscle and stamina. Ayrton Senna used to run in the heat of Brazil during the summer with a punishing four-day schedule of 8km, 16km, and 24km on successive days, followed by a rest day. Another former world champion, Jody Scheckter – top Grand Prix driver with Ferrari in 1979 – was so fit he won the World Superstar Championship in 1981, beating top-flight field athletes.

Double world champion Michael Schumacher plays football for a local team at his home near Zurich. Jacques Villeneuve, who won his first championship in 1997, loves to downhill race on skis, and four-times world champion Alain Prost was so fanatical about cycling that he used to compete in the pre-race mountain stages of the Tour de France. All Formula One drivers have their own gym, or access to one locally, and a private trainer whom the team retains for training sessions during the breaks between races and throughout the close season. British driver Johnny Herbert, for example, does at least two hours of cycling or gym work each day just to keep in trim. Then in January and February he will go and do some serious training with the team fitness coach, consisting largely of high-altitude cycling and cross-country skiing. Scottish driver David Coulthard works out for two hours a day at a gym below his apartment in Monaco and will take his personal fitness trainer with him to races.

Each driver also has his own dietician and team chefs prepare specialist menus on race weekends, observing strict guidelines. Pasta figures on most of the lunchtime team tables, as it is high in carbohydrates and protein and releases its energy slowly during periods of intense activity. One team doctor said that there were several important things to be aware of when preparing a driver's menu: 'Light and easy to digest, as race weekend stress puts strain on the digestive system. It is also important to select food that does not cause muscle strain or loss of concentration.'

There is no doubt at all that physical conditioning, together with the obviously vital ability to race a car, has a major effect on a driver's position on the grid. A driver needs crystal vision and reflexes poised on a hair trigger as he waits for the start, gunning his engine two seconds before the lights go off.

But still, no matter how fit a driver is, it remains inevitable that he will suffer emotional, mental and physical damage. Irrespective of how good a shape he's in, the immense stress of racing at 200 mph into a corner where some 20 other cars will be at roughly the same time and trying to avoid contact affects all drivers. Absolutely no one escapes. A driver will brake, accelerate, brake again, suffering three times his own body weight under gravitational load, steer to opposite lock, change gear half a dozen times, and watch cars both in front and behind. First corner safely negotiated, another 15 to go and then just 72 more laps.

And while all this is happening, strain on the heart and other parts of the body increases. The heart rate increases when working, approximately 25 beats per degree of body temperature increase, so the cooler one can remain in a heat load the less the strain on the heart: if the body temperature increases from 99°F to 103°F, this alone drives the pulse rate from 100 to 200 per minute. Despite the development of racing overalls that let air through more effectively, the temperature in the cockpit – especially in the pits when all the heat from the engine and the brakes, not just some of it, penetrates the compartment – often exceeds 100°F. Surrounding temperatures at recent Grand Prix races in countries such as Australia, Brazil, Portugal and Spain reached 110°F.

At Jacarepagua in 1982 surrounding temperatures hit the 123°F mark and the effect on three-times world champion Nelson Piquet, who collapsed on the podium due to dehydration and heat, was such that he needed intravenous fluid. Riccardo Patrese in the same race showed vagaries of performance caused by heat, when he was forced to retire after spinning and driving the wrong way.

Dehydration due to sweating can occur at the rate of 1.5 to 2 litres per hour in a man working at high surrounding temperatures so that in two hours up to 8.8lb (4kg) can be lost in body weight. Michael Schumacher lost approximately 12lb (5.5kg) at Interlagos, Brazil, in cool conditions, and several drivers reported regular losses of between 6 and 10lb (2.7 to 4.5 kg) in races during the 1998 Grand Prix season.

The average is only one or two kilos, which is far less than a few years ago in Formula One when a driver found it hard to drink during a race. Then he had to wait for a straight line to suck on a pipette but, by the time the liquid took to get to his mouth, he was already going round a bend. The centrifugal forces are such that it was impossible to drink and the liquid, a mixture of water and glucose, fell back into the flask until the next straight line when he tried again. Now, in most cars, an electric pump raises the liquid to the driver's lips and holds it in suspension in the pipette. He just needs to press a button to drink at once.

In 1983 Richalet and Bertrand estimated fluid loss in Formula One drivers to be between 0.5 and 1.0 litres (1kg) per hour of driving. It's less now, but still sufficient to lead to an increase of the blood cells in circulation, due to fluid loss. Losses of circulating sodium, potassium and magnesium also occur, along with increased production of certain hormones, including catecholamine, and cortisol and aldosterone from the adrenal glands as a biological response to counteract stress. As a result there is a severe reduction of urine production to conserve body fluid and at the end of the race it is not uncommon for a driver to have an empty bladder. On more than one occasion drivers are unable to provide a sample of urine for testing until they have been rehydrated. In 1982 the Medical Commission of FISA (Fédération Internationale de Sport Automobile) issued guidelines for diet and fluid management for racing in Formula One, recommending that one litre be taken before the race, one or two litres during the race and two litres afterwards – more than active infantry soldiers drank per hour to avoid dehydration during the Gulf War.

To a large extent this has alleviated the problem of severe dehydration, although drivers still experience uncomfortable levels of fluid loss. 'It's still a problem,' says McLaren driver David Coulthard. 'Weight loss can be as much as 6lb over the course of a race, most of it coming from fluid deprivation. Two litres is not an uncommon amount to sweat out in a cockpit and many a driver has collapsed before reaching the winner's podium. The more dehydrated you are, the more your performance starts to drop off. It's vital to keep your liquid levels up.'

This, however, is a minor problem compared to the physical damage caused by G-forces, vibration and several other factors. The G-forces alone are enough to cause severe muscular problems in later life, in fact several former Grand Prix drivers interviewed for this book reported restricted neck movement and severe pain in their shoulders, arms and upper back. It's no surprise, though, because it is widely accepted that the G-forces sustained by a driver while cornering, accelerating or braking provide stress, particularly on the muscles of the head, neck and shoulders, close to the edge of human tolerance.

Research carried out by FIA-appointed doctors and scientists have found 27 corners on Grand Prix circuits where the lateral G-forces are close to 4. This indicates that the driver's head plus helmet normally weighing 14lb (6.5kg) would under x4 G-forces represent a load of 57lb (26kg) to be controlled by the neck and shoulder muscles. Building up these muscles by exercise and weight training is a huge priority, but it doesn't always prevent muscular problems. Several drivers, including Damon Hill and Rubens Barrichello, have an uneven muscle distribution on their neck due to the constant pressures of driving on clockwise circuits. It is therefore extremely uncomfortable when the Grand Prix season arrives in Brazil and Japan, which are anti-clockwise, putting added strain on muscles that are used to a lesser degree during the season. 'I have a helmet with weights attached to the sides that I use to strengthen my neck,' says Hill. Other drivers such as Pedro Diniz lie on the floor and do 'head press-ups' with padded weights over their ears.

At circuits like Monaco, which are full of twists and turns, the lateral G-force is changing from side to side all the time and produces heavy work for the neck and shoulders, as well as exhaustion – remember Mansell falling all over the circuit at the end of the 1992 Monaco Grand Prix? And because the cars are now much quicker than ever before the problem is worse. Back in the early eighties Richalet and Bertrand plotted the pulse rate and G-forces under cornering, braking and accelerating, showing the heart rate going up to 178 during cornering while the G-forces on the corners reached 2.9 and during accelerating and braking fell from +1.1 to –2.8; a sum of changing G-force of 3.9. More than a decade later and the stress is much higher and physical damage more severe.

Vibration is another serious problem. Drivers have loosened teeth going over bumps, and taking the kerbing at the wrong angle can easily fracture ribs. Indeed, all the body parts get a pummelling over the course of a race. Vibration on the eye sockets can loosen contact lenses and cause sight fatigue; knees and elbows get knocked regularly. But this is nothing compared to spinal damage.

During a two-hour race the spine receives severe vertical loading as the result of the car bumping over irregularities in the surface of the circuit. This compresses and decompresses the intervertebral discs in the spine, which are made of fibrous and elastic material and act as the shock absorbing system. At the same time the spinal muscles are actively maintaining posture, counteracting G-forces and working constantly to minimize the vertical stretch and compression.

A.K. Burton, 'Back Pain in Grand Prix Drivers', *British Journal of Sports Medicine*, 17.150, 1983, and A.K. Burton and J. Sandover, 'Back Pain in Grand Prix Drivers: a "found" experiment', *Applied Ergonomics*, 18.1, 1987, revealed that changes in the suspension of Formula One cars between 1982 and 1983 significantly decreased the back pain and spinal damage occurring in the 15 Grand Prix drivers studied. In 1982 14 of the drivers complained of lumbar pain and 10 of neck pain, no driver being free from pain. The cars in 1982 had virtually no suspension, being ground-effect cars with high aerodynamic downforce and stiff suspension. But in 1983 FISA introduced rules reducing downforce with a 50 per cent reduction in the stiffness of the suspension. In 1983, as a result, only eight drivers had back pain and only seven neck pain, so almost half the drivers had no pain.

Nevertheless, many drivers today still have back and neck pain and X-rays of the spine of some current Formula One drivers show the unusual appearance of vertical disc protrusion. This and unavoidable wear on the neck due to vibration and G-forces leads to early arthritic change, and most drivers suffer, despite safeguards such as energy-absorbing padding and seats.

Bruising of the superficially lying nerves in drivers' arms and legs is also unavoidable. The tight constraints of the cockpit often lead to pressure and malfunction of the radial nerves, which run on the outside of the upper arm just below the shoulder. Several drivers, including Ayrton Senna, have experienced such problems in a race. In 1991 in Brazil at the end of the race, Senna was unable to get out of the car because his arms and hands were floppy and could not sustain his weight. Other drivers have reported losing power in their forearms so that their wrists go floppy during races.

In some of the worst cases, nerves on the outside of a driver's legs just below the knees (the lateral popliteal nerves) have been so damaged that both feet are temporarily paralysed. The palm of the hand and sole of the foot can sustain serious damage as well. Approximately 40lb of effort is required to turn a steering wheel at 170 mph and before the 'paddle' style semi-automatic gear levers were introduced, drivers had to perform manual sequential shifts that caused severe blistering and occasional bleeding of the palm, despite heavily padded racing gloves. Pressures on the sole of the foot due to heavy braking can cause constant pain throughout a race.

Olivier Panis (Prost-Peugeot 1998) says: 'The fact that semi-automatic gearboxes are now more common in F1 has not put an end to the pain that drivers used to suffer a few years ago, with blisters on the palms of their hands. It has not put an end to this pain, it has transferred it.

'Now we change up and down the gears by pressing our fingers on the levers located on each side of the steering wheel. At the end of the race, therefore, we have blisters on our fingertips. Our gloves are also made of Nomex, with a chamois leather covering to ensure a good grip on the wheel; sweat causes this leather to become very rough and the gloves lose their suppleness. Tactile perception is not as sensitive. So I change them after a Grand Prix.

'Helmet, overalls, gloves, boots, an F1 driver wears a new outfit for each race. This is not a question of style, but effectiveness. And the speed with which we wear out our clothes only emphasizes what a violent sport Formula One is. I wear out 12 pairs of racing shoes a year. It is sweat again and repeated impact, which wears away the soles. With carbon brakes, an F1 driver exerts such a muscular effort on his brake pedal that at the end of the Grand Prix he would suffer from an overheated arch if his shoes were not perfectly fitted to the shape of his foot.

'Our racing boots are like a boxer's boots: very supple to guarantee the foot's sensitivity, very narrow, as there is not much room inside the compartment, light and high. They are made of leather, covered with a Nomex skin.'

A Formula One driver may use as many as a dozen helmets in a season. That's almost a helmet for each of the 16 races in a Grand Prix year. With the heat, sweat and friction, the inner layer of the helmet expands quickly and does not hold the head as firmly. This is why a Formula One driver changes his helmet so often. After an accident, a helmet is systematically excluded for safety reasons, even if it was not directly hit, as its capacity for resistance may be reduced.

A technician is also present at every race just to prepare helmets. 'It's a vital process,' Panis says. 'Essentially it involves fitting the visors and the tear-offs, the thin, transparent films that cover the visor. We tear them off as we go round the circuit, when they become dirty from oil splashes and tyre rubber, so that we always have perfect visibility. I start with four tear-offs. I remove the first straight after the warm-up round, as the F1 engines give off oil when they start up on the grid. To remove a tear-off, you just need to pull a tab, which is either at its far left, or the far right.

'I always ask the technician to fit the three tear-offs that I remove during the race according to the same system: the first pulls off on the left, the second on the right, and the third on the left. In this way, when I come to remove a dirty tear-off, I don't need to wonder which hand to pull with, and I am certain not to pull off two at once. Our visors are very thick, four millimetres, as at 300km per hour the smallest bit of grit thrown up by your competitors' tyres can hit your helmet with the impact of a stone.'

A typical helmet weighs between 1 and 1.5 kg, including the radio. The mike that enables a driver to communicate with his pit during the race is built into the helmet. And the listening device goes into his earplugs. 'It is vital for us to hear the engine noise so we can detect any anomaly,' Panis points out. 'However a driver cannot drive an F1 car without protective earplugs. His eardrums would not stand it. I know this since in the past some drivers have gradually lost their hearing during their career. I regularly undergo tests.

'F1 drivers generally keep the same helmet colour throughout their careers. Maybe for some it is through superstition, but not in my case. A helmet, though, is like a driver's face. It is what the public sees and recognizes during the race. We can change the colour of our overalls, for instance, if we move from one team to another, but a driver never changes the colour of his helmet.'

After the helmet, comes the armour – the overalls – except that their aim is not to withstand impact, but rather fire, a driver's worst nightmare. The overalls are made of several layers of fireproof material, Nomex, and, to obtain authorization, must protect a driver for 12 seconds in a 700-degree hydrocarbon fire.

Panis added: 'Our overalls go from the feet up to the neck, and are very warm and thick. When I put mine on, I have the feeling I'm getting into a big cosy pair of pyjamas. I use two overalls for each Grand Prix weekend, so I can change them between the practice sessions. So I always have a clean, dry pair when I get into my car, which is a rather important element of comfort, as the overalls are soon soaked with sweat.'

Nigel Mansell drove a race with petrol leaking into his overalls causing extreme discomfort as it burned into his skin, and in Dallas in 1981 he even jumped out of his Lotus to push it over the line when he ran out of petrol on the last lap. The fact that he collapsed with the effort only lent weight to the degree of strength required to reach the chequered flag. A medical team found Mansell rolling around on the tarmac, physically intact but delirious.

'Exceptional skill and high motivation are significant factors in delaying or limiting deterioration in performance,' Mansell said, 'but in the end driving a Formula One car with virtually no suspension, under huge physical, mental and emotional strain, represents the limits of human tolerance. You really do go through hell for a couple of hours, but it's worth it for the buzz. It overrides everything, even the danger of death.'

# 4

# The Secret Side of Tazio Nuvolari

*One day, many years from now, the cost of our obsession with power and speed will be so high, the number of deaths, drivers and spectators, will be greater than the number of champions. People will look back and say 'Is it worth it?' but men will still race cars because some of us are born to it, and destined to die doing it.*

TAZIO NUVOLARI, 1952

All of those who choose to compete in Formula One – indeed in any kind of motor racing – face the real possibility of serious injury or death. Those who take part in this deadly pursuit are acutely aware of the hazards involved, even if they are not afraid to face them. As Gilles Villeneuve once quipped: 'Sure, death could be waiting around the next corner, but I'm not about to stop and introduce myself. I control the risks, minimize the danger, so death becomes only a remote possibility.'

But it was this slight chance that killed Villeneuve. Death was not only waiting around the next corner at Zolder, it was riding in his Ferrari with him. That is why, despite the enormous strides made in car construction and circuit safety, accidents can and will still happen, largely because men who drive racing cars tempt fate, and the memories of the dreadful fatal accidents that darkened past races are burned into the minds of the entire motor racing world.

Italian driver Tazio Nuvolari, a legend in his own lifetime, tempted fate with a passion, but in 1952, a year before his death, Nuvolari made a chilling prediction: 'We [the drivers] spin the wheel of fate,' he said, 'with no regard for the consequences. Most of us don't care if we live or die as long as there is glory. One day many years from now, the cost of our obsession will be so high, the number of deaths, drivers and spectators, will be greater than the number of champions. People will look back and say "Is it worth it?" but men will still race cars because some of us are born to it, and destined to die doing it.'

Three years later, at 4 p.m. on 11 June 1955 at Le Mans, France, the race that would witness the worst disaster in motor racing began. Nuvolari's prediction was about to come true. Shortly before the first pit stops the Mercedes of Pierre Levegh hit the Austin-Healey of British driver Macklin at over 130 mph and launched into the air, landing on the earthen barrier that divided the spectators from the pit straight. The car burst into flames and the shock of the crash tore out the engine and front suspension which hurtled into the trapped crowd, killing 83 people and injuring over 100.

Almost half a century later, at the end of the 1998 Grand Prix season, the total number of fatalities, including drivers, officials and spectators, numbered more than 300; an average of three a year since the French held the very first Grand Prix near Le Mans in 1906. Down the halls of consequence, the echo of Nuvolari's words never fades. His philosophy was ruthlessly simple, just like the deadly game of power and speed he loved to play: no guts, no glory.

The Flying Mantuan, as Nuvolari became known, epitomized courage and daring and for 30 years he amazed the racing world with his exploits. He loved to drive very fast, in fact he raced with such wild abandon that, by the time his light went out, his body had been patched up more times than the cars he used to wreck. Nuvolari frequently came back from serious injury only to compete in bandages, but he was good even when he was on his last legs.

In his entire career the Italian won almost 200 major races and came second only 17 times, and with his rugged film star looks and seductive personality, Nuvolari had a reputation as a daredevil playboy; he had balls in more ways than one. But he had a secret side; deeply religious and superstitious, he would pray often – significantly before every race towards the end of his career – even though he had something of a fatalist approach to racing. 'When my time is up, that will be it,' he said. 'It's no good worrying about being killed on the track. I understand the risks and accept the danger, just as I accept my own mortality.'

A priest who was a friend of the Nuvolari family chastised Tazio for his love of motor racing. 'You should do something more worthwhile with your life,' he told the Italian during the early days of his vibrant career. 'Why tempt fate?'

Nuvolari, who had great respect for the Roman Catholic church, thought for a moment before replying: 'You are wrong, Father,' he said. 'I don't tempt fate, I embrace life. I love God and I love life. Motor racing is my life and there is no sin in that.'

Nuvolari was born on 18 November 1892, in Casteldrio near Mantua. His Uncle Giuseppe was a Bianchi dealer and introduced his nephew to motor sports. After serving in the Italian army as a driver he started racing motorcycles seriously when he was 28. He raced Nortons, Saroleas, Garellis, Fongris and Indians. The powerful Bianchi team noticed his riding and he became a member and eventually Italian champion.

At the Monza Grand Prix for motorcycles he crashed during practice. This resulted in two broken legs. After doctors put plaster casts on both legs he was told that it would be at least one month before he could walk again, let alone race motorcycles. The next day he started the race having himself tied to his bike. He required his mechanics to hold him upright at the start of the race and to catch him at the end. The legend of Tazio Nuvolari was born that day when he won the race.

Nuvolari began racing cars in 1924 at the age of 32 while still competing on motorcycles. In 1927 he started his own team, buying a pair of Bugatti 35Bs which he shared with his partner Achille Varzi, who was also a successful motorcycle racer. This partnership would later turn into an intense rivalry. Nuvolari began to win races at the expense of Varzi who left the team. Varzi, the son of a wealthy merchant, could afford better equipment and bought an Alfa P2, with which he had the better of Nuvolari. Tazio himself signed on with Alfa Romeo in 1929 and was a team-mate of his rival Varzi once again.

The renowned Mille Miglia, run over public roads closed for 24 hours, amounted to a 1,000-mile lap of Italy. The 1930 race went down in history when Nuvolari caught an unsuspecting Varzi while driving in the night with no headlights. Three kilometres from the finish he suddenly pulled alongside; smiling at his startled team-mate he flicked on his headlights and powered on to victory.

For the Targa Floria of 1932 he requested of Enzo Ferrari a mechanic who weighed as little or less than he did. Nuvolari took the young and inexperienced mechanic that Ferrari had given him and told him that he would warn him when they approached a particularly difficult corner so as not to unduly frighten the young man. As they approached a corner, Nuvolari would shout for the mechanic to take cover under the dashboard. After the race and another victory for Nuvolari, Ferrari asked the mechanic how he had made out. 'Nuvolari started shouting at the first bend and finished at the last one,' the boy answered. 'I was down at the bottom of the car all the time.'

In 1933 he scored many victories but became estranged from the team manager Enzo Ferrari and left for Maserati. 1933 also saw him travel to Northern Ireland for the Tourist Trophy Race and a drive in a supercharged MG K3 Magnette. After his total domination of the race someone asked him if he liked the MG's brakes. Nuvolari replied that he couldn't really tell, he hadn't used them that much. In 1935 he was induced to return to Alfa Romeo and scored one of his greatest victories at the Nurburgring, driving an obsolete Alfa against the might of the German nation. He drove at the ragged edge and sometimes over it. His relentless pursuit caused the lead Mercedes to retire with a blown tyre and he cruised to victory in front of a large gathering of Nazi party officials.

In 1936 he had a serious accident during practice for the Tripoli Grand Prix but escaped from the hospital and took a taxi to the race where he finished seventh in a spare car. After the death of Bernd Rosemeyer in 1938, Auto Union was desperate for a driver who could master their mid-engine race car. At the insistence of Dr Ferdinand Porsche they turned to an Italian, Nuvolari, who would go on to win the British Grand Prix at Donington.

Only World War Two could halt Nuvolari's progress but after the fighting stopped he returned to racing at the age of 53. In a minor race he had the steering wheel come off his car yet managed to return to the pits holding the wheel in one hand and the steering column with the other. He continued to win but age and sickness from acute asthma, the result of years of inhaling exhaust fumes, were finally taking their toll.

His last Mille Miglia, in 1948, was a defining moment in his illustrious career. It was said that he wanted to die in the sport that he loved so much but in this wish he was denied. On 11 August 1953, nine months after suffering a paralysing stroke, he was dead. As was his wish, he was buried in his uniform – the yellow jersey and blue trousers.

More than 50,000 people attended his funeral. Enzo Ferrari, arriving in Mantua, stopped at a plumber's shop to ask for directions. Seeing the Modena licence plates and unaware of the identity of the driver, the workman murmured, 'Thank you for coming. A man like that won't be born again.' The irony would not have been lost on Nuvolari. Even in death he embraced life.

# 5

# Smiling in the Face of Danger

*People say I drive like a madman, on and off the track. They say I'm insane because I smile when faced with danger. Maybe I am a little crazy, but let me tell you something else – I'll die a happy man because doing what I do makes me feel alive.*

GILLES VILLENEUVE, TWO YEARS BEFORE HIS DEATH IN 1982

Juan Manuel Fangio, one of the all-time great racing drivers, was a 'religious man who feared God, prayed often, and sinned even more often'. This, of course, was Fangio's view of himself, years before he died and years before his faith became very important to him. 'I am,' he said, 'a deeply flawed human being and God should know because he made me. It is probably why I was born to race cars; so I could never have any illusions about my own mortality – always knowing one mistake could end it all.'

Fangio, who died in a Buenos Aires hospital on the morning of Monday 17 July 1995, was no ordinary man, no ordinary sportsman. He was loved the world over, respected and revered by his team-mates and competitors alike and universally accepted as the greatest motor racing driver of all time. He was the Pele or Ali of motor racing, he had charisma, brilliance, courage – one of the immortals. As British racing legend Stirling Moss put it, after hearing the sad news of his greatest friend and fellow driver, he was 'a gentleman, not of birth, but of being'.

In his book *Racers*, sportswriter Richard Williams describes Fangio as 'symbolizing the heroic age when racing drivers went about their business in cork helmets, polo shirts, string-backed gloves and suede loafers, forearms bare to the wind, faces streaked with hot oil. It was an age when chivalry still played a part and when the physical danger was such that each race seemed to thin the ranks of the participants. Perhaps the two were not unconnected.'

'The maestro', as he was respectfully known, was 84 when his wonderful life as motor racing's greatest champion sadly ran out of road. The news of his death stunned the sport, even though he was known to be suffering from ill health. He had already survived several heart attacks and was being treated for serious medical conditions, but no other announcement could have brought such instant sobriety, except perhaps the tragic death of Ayrton Senna at the age of 34. Senna, regarded by many as the greatest Grand Prix driver of the modern era, had won three world championships; but Fangio, who did not race in his first Grand Prix until he was 38, won five.

Fangio was born in Balcarce, an Argentinian potato town, in 1911. He was the son of a stonemason from a family of Italian immigrants who built a monumental achievement in sporting history. Symbolically, Argentina had held its first motor race in the year before Juan's birth. At the age of four he was enthralled by a neighbour's single-cylinder machine, and at 10 he was hanging around the garage of a Senor Capettini, fetching and carrying tools for the mechanics and driving a car, a chain-driven Panhard-Levassor, for the first time. By his mid-teens he was volunteering to deliver cars for customers and ascribed his famous skill in slippery conditions to his early experience of driving on muddy tracks, which encouraged him to learn a delicate touch.

Soon after his 10th birthday Fangio took part in his first race, as the riding mechanic in a four-cylinder Plymouth driven by one of Vigiano's customers. His first real competitive race, though, was in a converted taxi in 1936, his first victory on a long-distance endurance event in 1940 and his first Grand Prix, in Europe, in 1950 at Reims.

At an age when most men are ready to retire from racing, Fangio's career began and took off, carrying him to such heights that his achievements remain untouched today. Every driver to win a race since 1950 has been in awe of him and his feats with Alfa Romeo, Maserati, Mercedes Benz and Ferrari. Jackie Stewart once said: 'When Fangio comes in to a room the conversation stops. You hear us all just whispering about him. Everything else is forgotten.'

Fangio survived in an era when death was a constant unwanted companion. He said in 1990: 'In my 10 years of driving in Europe,

I saw 30 of my friends and rivals killed.' Fangio had two dreadful accidents. The first was in 1948, late at night while competing in the epic Gran Premio de la America del Sur in Argentina, when he missed a corner and went off the road, rolling his old Chevrolet car. His co-driver Daniel Urrutia was killed.

Four years later, during the winter of 1952, Fangio accepted an offer to drive for Maserati. It was to be his worst season and almost ended in tragedy thanks to the events of a June weekend. On the Saturday he was due to race a BRM in the Ulster Trophy race on the Dundrod circuit near Belfast, followed on the Sunday by his first race in the Maserati, in the Monza Grand Prix. After the BRM's retirement he flew from Belfast to Paris, there to be told that bad weather had ruled out all flights to Italy. Undeterred, Fangio drove non-stop through the night to Monza, just northeast of Milan, arriving two hours before the race was due to start.

'You look a bit tired,' one of the Maserati team told him. 'Oh, it's nothing,' Fangio replied. But after starting from the grid in an unfamiliar car, he misjudged the Seraglio curve on the second lap and woke up in hospital with broken vertebrae. It put him out for more than a year. 'It was a short story,' he said. 'I arrived at two. I raced at two-thirty and I was in hospital with a broken neck by three.'

Fangio said once: 'Fear is not a stupid thing. Winning is not a question of courage, but of faith in oneself and in the car. A car is like a creature that lives, with its own emotions and its own heart. You have to understand it and to live it accordingly. I knew many drivers more courageous than me. They are dead now.'

He was famed for more than his racing. Stories of his love affairs were frequent, including one with the actress Gina Lollobrigida, but it will be for his racing that he is remembered. His greatest win was in the German Grand Prix at the Nurburgring in 1957, when he was driving for Maserati. He gambled victory on a pit stop for fuel and tyres, but rejoined 48 seconds behind.

'It was a marvellous, great moment,' said Stirling Moss, who was watching. 'He caught the two Ferraris and then he passed Mike Hawthorn on one side and Peter Collins on the other, behind the pits. It was a masterly move.' Fangio, who broke the lap record 10 times to win by 3.6 seconds, said: 'I was inspired that day. I never quite drove like that before and never drove like it again.'

Motor racing was his first love for a long time and even when he wasn't competing, Fangio loved nothing better than racing along the country roads near his home in Argentina, especially if he had company. In this respect Fangio has something in common with Gilles Villeneuve who used to get a kick from watching passengers in his car squirm in their seats as he hurtled along city streets, dodging lamp posts and trucks and running red lights, and sending dust and gravel spraying into thin air as his screeching tyres hugged the narrowest of mountain rims.

Fangio, just short of his 80th birthday, spun his Mercedes off the road at over 100 mph to avoid an oncoming truck. His passengers reported that Fangio just smiled and carried on. The experience would have given him an immense thrill, simply because he was so in control of the car that he could have done it a hundred times with equal flair and precision.

Towards the close of his life, though, as the end of life's great open road loomed, Fangio focused more on his faith in personal beliefs and less on the thrills and spills of his only true love. The irony is this: Juan Manuel Fangio believed he would die a violent and glorious death at the wheel of a race car. He never wanted to die of old age in a hospital bed. But when he did, he had more peace and less fear of death than at any time during his Grand Prix career.

# 6

# Blow-out

*Once you sit in a racing car you know you are taking risks. We never think we are going to have an accident or get hurt but it is always at the back of the mind. It is that knowledge which determines the limit you establish for yourself.*

AYRTON SENNA

Seven years before his death, Jim Clark provided a poignant insight into what motivates men who drive racing cars. There is nothing fancy about Clark's words and his plain truth only states the obvious, but what he did is open up the mind of the racing driver with a natural honesty as compelling as the magnetism of sport and risk that makes up the world of motor racing which killed him in the end.

This pragmatic, God-fearing Scotsman best sums up the need for speed, rather like British explorer George Mallory who, when asked why he wanted to climb Mount Everest, replied: 'Because it is there.' Clark would have said the same thing. He raced cars because they were there. 'It's no great mystery,' he said. 'And I don't need a psychiatrist or a priest to tell me why I do what I do. Men who drive racing cars do it because they can. That's all it is. Sorry to disappoint you but there is no great secret about my profession, it's simply an extension of what most men become whenever they get behind the wheel of an ordinary car. The power and speed makes us feel good, gives us a thrill and a sense of being extraordinary.

'But the bottom line is, if cars didn't exist men would race horse and cart, and if the wheel had never been invented, man would just race horses or each other. It's a natural instinct, only technology has transformed this need for speed into a potentially deadly pursuit.'

When he died in 1968 on the Hockenheim track in West Germany Jim Clark had won more Grand Prix races than anyone else, and had been the world champion twice over. His versatility at the wheel embraced cars of all sorts, for his enthusiasm was boundless in a sport which even then was becoming deeply professional. The fame and fortune of his short life, flying his own Twin Comanche before he died at the age of 32, contrasted with his Presbyterian upbringing, although he often used to say that one day he would go back to the farm in Kilmaddy, in the county of Fife; the place where he was born and raised by a Scottish farming family, roots that would stay with him the rest of his life.

Sadly, he never had the opportunity. A blow-out in a tyre threw his Lotus off course during an unimportant Formula Two race, in which he took part owing to what amounted to a clerical error, and which he had no chance of winning. His collision with a tree shocked the motor racing world. Jim Clark had fewer doubts about his job right until the last moments of his life than Senna, Ratzenberger, Gilles Villeneuve, Nuvolari and others, but strangely he began to read his Bible and pray more often during the weeks leading up to his accident at Hockenheim.

Whether he suddenly became more aware of his own mortality or began to question the sense of risking his life is open to debate but one thing is clear: in 1967, roughly six months before the end of his life, Clark started to lose faith in the idea that a driver could be skilful enough to outwit death on the track. Before a race at Monaco he admitted: 'Sometimes I question the sense of it all. Speed kills and yet I live for speed. One day I'm going to walk away from all of this, while I still can. Because one thing is certain, the law of averages says that sooner or later I'm going to have an accident irrespective of how good a driver I am. It happens to the best.'

Clark had several lucky escapes before he died. In fact, by the time he set out at Hockenheim on that fateful afternoon in April 1968, he had become well acquainted with death on the track. In 1960 at Spa in Belgium – the nine-mile monster widely regarded as the most dangerous course in Grand Prix racing – Clark's teammate Alan Stacey died. Badly shaken by the experience, Clark was reduced to tears but still managed to finish fifth in only his second Grand Prix.

His first race for Lotus had been at the Dutch Grand Prix in 1960, where he raced in place of John Surtees who was still racing motorcycles at the time. His race was pretty uneventful as he worked his way up to fifth place before having to retire with a seized gearbox.

A year later at the Italian Grand Prix, Clark's Lotus came into contact with the Ferrari of Wolfgang von Trips. The Ferrari was propelled into the crowd, killing several spectators as well as the German driver. Once again Clark was badly shaken and spent a long, troubled night wondering whether to quit. He didn't and went on to dominate the world championship, although one gets the impression that Jim Clark would have been much happier sticking to racing his not-too-extravagant Sunbeams and TR2s along the twisting Border roads of his youth. In fact the real truth is that he came close to turning his back on Formula One racing because of the danger. 'Don't tempt fate,' his mother would warn him, but like a true boy racer Jim just had to get behind the wheel.

He was the only son in a family of four daughters and his early racing exploits were initially met by family disapproval. He raced in rallies and other local races under the guidance of his friend Ian Scott-Watson. Later he joined a team run by Jock McBain known as the Border Reivers. In one of these races he drove a Lotus Elite against none other than Colin Chapman, head of the Lotus team. Chapman was very impressed by the young Scotsman and he would keep an eye on this young lad. Ironically, in 1959 the Border Reivers planned to buy a single-seater Formula Two Lotus for Clark but after watching Graham Hill lose a wheel in a similar car, Clark decided that the Lotus cars were unsafe and that he would stick to sports cars for the time being.

Eventually he graduated to an Aston Martin which brought him to the attention of Reg Parnell, the factory team manager. Aston Martin was planning on entering Formula One and after a test he signed the young Scotsman. Clark had also by this time signed a Formula Two contract with Colin Chapman's Lotus. Aston Martin's Formula One car was a disaster and the factory decided to abandon its efforts. In Formula Two Clark enjoyed immediate success and when the Aston Martin drive failed to materialize, Clark signed on with Lotus for Formula One as well. In 1963 Clark dominated the world championship, winning an amazing seven out of 10 races, recording seven pole positions in the process. In 1968 he started the season with a win in South Africa, which allowed him to surpass Juan Manuel Fangio in Grand Prix victories. But this was to be his last win and the very last time he would 'tempt fate'.

Clark's greatness lies less in his performances at the wheel and more in the affection of a motor racing generation. According to those who knew him, Jim Clark was simply 'one of the boys'. He had a knack of bringing Grand Prix racing down to earth, making it accessible to the average guy in the street. 'Oh sure, you could do it, no problem,' he'd tell his friends. 'There's nothing to it. Any one of you boys could do what I'm doing – in fact some of you are probably better drivers.'

Motor racing correspondent Eric Dymock wrote in the *Guardian* in 1978:

*[Jim Clark] was that rare public person whose constancy was real and obvious. His warmth was genuine, and his reserve reflected no more than a natural Scottish concern over the danger of being taken for a ride. Clark never lost any friends on his way to the top, remaining essentially the same agreeable Border lad, brought up in a wealthy farm community, able to indulge his taste for fast sporty cars. But he was gifted with the quick sportsman's wit that enabled him to process information from his hand and eye and drive a car with a skill and bearing that astonished his contemporaries.*

It was perception, not simply a keen eye; poise, not just balance; the right reaction, and not just the quick reaction that added up to the qualities that distinguish the natural driver from the merely well trained. Clark possessed them to the degree that, if he was not fastest in practice, or leading the race, there was something wrong with his car – something seriously wrong because a minor fault, like the suspension rod that hung off for most of the race at Monaco in 1964, he would adjust for himself.

Clark insisted that 'anyone could do my job, if he put his mind to it', but that was Clark just being modest. Maybe he believed it in part, because he was such an unassuming, level-headed kind of guy, but in reality you've got to be a bit special to drive a racing car. It takes supreme skill, natural ability, guts and nerves of steel, and faith – faith in personal beliefs.

Some drivers have faith in their power to be adroit enough to outwit death, or – to put it another way – good enough behind the wheel to escape their own mortality; others have faith in the 'wheel of life', as Gilles Villeneuve put it, accepting death as one possible outcome of their chosen game, but doing all they possibly can to avoid it for as long as they possibly can. Some, like Jim Clark, and later Ayrton Senna, have faith in God, but even the greatest power in the universe cannot interfere with the law of averages. 'It's a sobering truth,' Clark said. 'I believe in God but I choose to risk my life so I can't blame Him if something happens to me. I'll only have myself to blame.'

## 7

# The Williamson Incident

*I'll never be a bloody saint but when you live in the fast lane of life it pays to know who your maker is. You never know when your time is going to be up. I could be knocking on the gates tomorrow.*

DAVID PURLEY, 1984, 12 MONTHS BEFORE HIS DEATH

David Purley had, in his own words, 'my own special relationship with God'. 'I'm not religious, in the true sense of the word, and I'm not particularly fond of church. I don't pray much, or read the Bible. But I believe in God and He knows I do. I keep the faith inside, in my heart of hearts.'

'Godly' is not a word that springs to mind when describing Purley. He rarely spared a thought for the 'maker', as he occasionally referred to God; neither did he have much time for those who did. Former paratrooper, millionaire's son, amateur racer and braver than Biggles, Purley was a lovely guy with the heart of a lion. He was also a fiery competitor who did not suffer fools easily and had a reputation for verbally abusing anyone who upset him, irrespective of their reputation.

The most famous example of Purley's conversational firepower is his heated exchange with former world champion Niki Lauda. The occasion was the 1977 Belgian Grand Prix at Zolder. Lauda blamed Purley, driving his home-brewed Lec CRP1 on its race debut, for holding him up as the British driver led the chaotic rain-soaked race for a fleeting but nevertheless glorious half-lap. 'You bloody rabbits should not be allowed in these races,' fumed Lauda, wagging his finger at Purley with uncharacteristic loss of composure.

Purley's response is legendary: 'You wag your finger at me one more time, I'm going to break it off and stick it right up your arse!' Lauda was speechless and at the next Grand Prix, Purley teased the Austrian by racing with the profile of a rabbit stuck on the Lec's cockpit sides. It was his way of bringing Grand Prix racing down to his own gritty, unpretentious level.

But if there is a reward for courage and integrity then Purley will be in heaven. God loves an honest man and David Purley was honest as the day is long. He was a man born out of his time. A generation earlier he would surely have been in the thick of the Battle of Britain action. He served with the Marines in Aden, was a ferociously competitive Formula Three racer and earned a George Medal for his heroic, yet sadly vain, attempts to rescue fellow March driver Roger Williamson from an upturned blazing car in the 1973 Dutch Grand Prix.

Twelve years on Purley met his death, just off Bognor Regis promenade, when the plane he was flying plunged into the Channel just after he'd 'beaten up' the seafront, a trick he learned as a teenager. He was just 40 years old.

The son of the owner of Lec Refrigeration, which became one of Britain's most successful fridge makers, Purley graduated to Formula Three in 1970 with a Brabham BT28. He put his name on the map as a man to watch when he beat James Hunt's Lotus 59 to a split-second victory in the Grand Prix des Frontières on the Chimay road circuit in Belgium. Hunt was a brutally tough Formula Three competitor at that time, but Purley refused to concede defeat and got the better of him. He also returned to Chimay in 1971 and 1972 driving for Brabham and Ensign respectively, to complete a hat-trick of victories.

Hunt later recalled: 'David Purley was a brave, brave racing driver. He was not everyone's cup of tea but he was a decent man, an honest competitor who always gave his all and genuinely loved the sport. He was very serious about racing.'

But Purley was also frustrated that some people did not take him seriously and this, coupled with a desperate need to prove himself because of his often overpowering father, created a do-or-die attitude. He was always prepared to take the extra risk to succeed.

In 1973, Purley decided to move up and have a go at Formula One with a March 731, not the most reliable of racing cars. Practising for the British Grand Prix at Silverstone, a brake problem put him into the bank at Becketts and he was forced to withdraw because of a damaged chassis. The car was repaired in time for the Dutch race at Zandvoort where he qualified 21st, 0.4 seconds behind the works March 731 driven by his old Formula Three sparring partner, Roger Williamson.

Tragedy struck midway round the eighth lap with the two of them running in close company, in 13th and 14th. Williamson had gone off the road on a long, fifth gear right-hander and slammed into the guard rail. The works March was flipped into the air, flew for about 80 yards, and then crashed back down on to the track. Upside down, it then caught fire.

What followed was one of the most disreputable episodes Formula One has ever delivered for public consumption. It left a stain on the sport for all time, although many of those who follow motor racing in the glitzy, showbiz present, will probably not even spare a thought for the shocking way a driver was allowed to die almost 30 years ago.

As Purley wrestled to right the upturned March, the rest of the field passed the spot time and time again. Nobody stopped to help. Afterwards some of the drivers felt 'sick with guilt' that nobody had given Purley a hand. But it was too late. The whole sequence of events, together with Purley's overwhelming despair, was witnessed live on television. Purley never completely got over it. He had seen death and destruction while serving with the Marines in Aden – on one occasion he was the sole survivor of an armoured car crew which ran over a mine – yet the Williamson incident had a profound effect on him.

Physically, apart from ruptured blood vessels down the inside of his arms, he survived the harrowing experience largely intact. Emotionally, though, he was shattered. It was a hellish thing to see a man burnt alive. In those horrifying moments of despair, Purley prayed for the strength of ten men. Afterwards he prayed for peace of mind, but the memory haunted him for years.

In 1974 Purley returned to Formula Two, driving March and Chevron cars for a private team. It was a successful season; three second places helped Purley to fifth spot in the European Formula Two championship, trailing men such as Jacques Laffite and Patrick Depailler who went on to make their names in Formula One.

The return to Grand Prix racing came in 1977 with the Lec CRP1, its designation based on Charlie Purley's initials. In qualifying for its first Grand Prix at Zolder the Lec was hampered by fuel problems. After taking 13th place, David Purley struggled to 14th in the Swedish Grand Prix at Anderstorp, then spun off due to brake failure in the French race at Dijon-Prenois. It was a lucky escape and a warning. Then came disaster.

During pre-qualifying for the British Grand Prix at Silverstone, the problematic Lec suffered an engine fire. It had been doused with extinguishant which, unbeknown to the team or Purley, had clogged up the throttle mechanism. It jammed open and the Lec slammed into the bank at Becketts at around 100 mph. The impact stopped the car within five feet, giving Purley an entry in the *Guinness Book of Records* as surviving the most destructive accident ever recorded.

Purley was almost completely crushed by the impact. He suffered 17 breaks in each leg and a triple fracture of his pelvis. It was a miracle he survived at all and recuperation took more than a year. Eventually Purley forced himself back into the cockpit but his comeback was short-lived. The physical effort involved was enormous and he would battle the discomfort of those Silverstone injuries for the rest of his life. That too was short-lived. Turning back to his first love, flying, David Purley lost control of his Pitts Special biplane and dived into the sea on 2 July 1985. His time was up.

## 8

# Good Flight Plan, Bad Landing

*Only a fool would risk his life for a living and not have some faith in God.*

MARIO ANDRETTI

'Death,' whispered Mario Andretti, 'is a great leveller. Everyone dies, even sporting legends. No one is too rich, or too famous, or too important; no one is exempt, no one escapes.'

Andretti, famous for his more light-hearted and laconic one-liners, frowned. He thought for a moment and added: 'Motor racing is a deadly occupation because death is always on the agenda. Time and time again people ask, "Do you worry about being killed?" Of course not, because in this profession you cannot afford to dwell on such things. Men who drive racing cars die; it's a fact. But most of us live to a ripe old age.'

That is also a fact. There are many, many more ex-Grand Prix drivers soaking up the sun in wealthy retirement than graves of those who died on the track. The survival rate is very high and most drivers have a laid-back philosophy about the risks involved. 'If it happens, it happens. But with a lot of skill and a little luck it won't,' is the general feeling.

But strangely, and according to Andretti, death is one of the very reasons why men become great racing car drivers. In this deadly game of high-speed risk, death is transformed from equalizer to catalyst. Instead of making men equal it separates mere mortals from gods; elevates men to high places where legends are born. Remember the words of Tazio Nuvolari: 'You can't be afraid of death and be a great racing car driver.'

There is an element of truth in this even though it is a sad irony, because in the end Nuvolari deeply feared his own mortality. Maybe, as the theme of this book suggests, when racing car drivers begin to fear death then it is time for them to quit. It is a natural warning, a built-in alarm clock; the changing of a season. It happens to us all, but not all of us live on the edge where life and death are separated by the thinnest of lines – a borderline blurred by power and speed and ambition.

Once upon a time Mario Andretti stuck a nonchalant, rude finger up to death, but maybe as you get older you become less willing to tempt fate; you don't have to be old to be wise, so the saying goes, but with age comes respect and, according to Andretti, 'You realize that you are not invincible, not a super-hero, and not above the law of averages or physics. Racing drivers take risks, risks cause accidents, and accidents can prove fatal.

'I'm not saying motor racing is like a game of Russian roulette, because we do everything we can to control and minimize the risks involved, but sooner or later ... BANG! Someone gets whacked. It happens.'

This real danger keeps racing drivers on their toes. Death is a present threat, a permanent shadow. But once you've faced it – looked it right in the eye – and learned to survive and thrive right on the edge of that thin borderline, to remain fearless while knowing that one mistake or twist of cruel fate or bad luck could end it all in an instant, then you earn the right to become a legend.

Mario Andretti's place in the motor racing hall of fame is secure. He is not afraid of death but there have been times in his life when the fragility of human existence has been brought sharply into focus. On more than one occasion Andretti, arguably one of the greatest ever racing drivers, has questioned the sense of it all, but, like a true speed king, he has been unable to resist the gripping attraction of risk and sport that makes up motor racing, even though it has killed some of his closest friends and wounded his big brave Italian heart.

There was never a man who loved racing more than Mario Andretti, and there was never a man who knew its dangers more than he did. 'I always felt I was put on this earth to drive race cars,' he says, 'and maybe I'll die for the same reason. Speed thrills and kills, with equal measure.'

The mere mention of his name conjures up an image of speed, just as the proverbial sarcasm, 'Who do you think you are, Mario

Andretti?' has been heard from the lips of police officers and back seat drivers alike. The computer spell checker knows who he is. Even people with only a hazy awareness of the sport of motor racing recognize Andretti as the very essence of the professional race car driver. A driver who has won on everything with four wheels.

He was born in Montona, Italy, on 28 February 1940, just three months before Mussolini worked up the courage to throw in his lot with Hitler, and thrust Italy into World War Two. At the cessation of hostilities the Andrettis found that their homeland was destined to become part of postwar Yugoslavia. They became refugees from Communism, spending several years in a camp at Tuscani.

Andretti caught the motor racing bug when he was a young boy watching the Mille Miglia from his front gate. Until its demise in 1957, the Mille Miglia was the greatest free show in motor racing and virtually everyone turned out to watch. Stirling Moss's Mercedes Benz won in May 1955, and his average speed, a trace away from 98 mph, still stands as the fastest over the course. Many Italians, children at the time, including Andretti, remember the silver car hurtling by.

In 1954 Mario's interest in motor racing was quickened by a visit to Monza to see the great Ascari compete in the Italian Grand Prix. It was an emotive experience but for 15-year-old Andretti the excitement later gave way to tears. He was about to leave with his family for a new life in the USA and recalls: 'In my own mind I had seen racing cars for the last time. So far as I knew, the only race over there was the Indianapolis 500. I understood we had to go to the States – Italy sure as hell wasn't offering us much – but I was obsessed with being a racing driver, and it seemed like I was kissing it goodbye.'

He couldn't have been further from the truth. Contrary to what he had believed, the United States was alive with motor racing. What's more, it was a much less elitist sport than in Europe, so there were ways into it for a poor kid bursting with ambition.

In 1955 his family emigrated to the United States, making their new home in Nazareth, Pennsylvania. Andretti soon made his mark, talking his way into drives in the murderously dangerous sprint cars. 'You had to drive those things very desperately,' he says, 'but I didn't give a thought to safety back then. Guys were getting killed all the time, but the words were never used: they always "bought the farm"...'

When Mario started racing on dirt ovals around Nazareth in 1959 in an old Hudson, he was not the only racing Andretti. His twin brother, Aldo, competed on the same tracks, indeed in the same car. Unfortunately, an accident put a premature end to Aldo's career. Mario, however, kept on. On a single autumn day in 1963 he won three midget races on two separate tracks. In 1964 he began competing in USAC sprint car and Indycar races. He had the maturity to turn down an Indianapolis 500 ride that year, feeling that he needed more racing experience. When he did enter the Big Race for the first time the next year, he took third and Rookie of the Year honours.

Mark Twain is said to have agreed with the aphorism that if at first you don't succeed, try, try again, with the qualification that after that you should quit – there's no sense making a damn fool of yourself. Andretti achieved success at Indy early, winning it on his fifth try in 1969. After that he tried and tried for more than 20 years to win it a second time, but was never again successful. He was actually declared the winner briefly one year following some scoring confusion, but the race was ultimately awarded to Bobby Unser. Andretti's Indianapolis career may not be evidence cited by those who believe that dogged persistence always pays off.

But it is a testament to his versatility and completeness as a driver that he is not remembered today as the poor sucker who beat his head in vain against the brickyard all those years, but rather for his wide-ranging success almost everywhere, including Indianapolis.

Andretti was already a Daytona 500 winner, Sebring winner, two-time USAC champion and four-time Indianapolis 500 competitor when he entered his first Formula One race. It was in 1968 at Watkins Glen in a Lotus 49B, and it promised great things, to say the least. Much to the chagrin of his competitors he took pole position. Oh, sure, they said. It's his home track. Actually he had never driven at the Glen before.

Unfortunately, he did not finish as his Lotus more or less fell apart under him. In fact his whole 1969 season, a grand total of three races, was one frustrating unfinished race after another. Of course, that year he was busy elsewhere, winning the 500, the USAC championship for a third time and the Pikes Peak Hill Climb.

It was Colin Chapman who first began to spread the word about Mario. The Lotus boss had taken his team to Indianapolis, seen this skinny kid run there, and been much impressed. And when Jim Clark was killed early in 1968, Chapman concluded that Andretti was the man to replace him.

Both Clark and Andretti loved to fly; Clark in his own Twin Comanche and Andretti in anything quick and powerful. Ironically, both men were more afraid of being killed in a plane crash than a car wreck. During many of his Formula One years, Andretti was a Concorde commuter, shuttling back and forth across the Atlantic at a dizzying pace in order to compete both in Grand Prix and in USAC events. This necessarily caused him to miss some F1 races each season through 1972, eliminating any chance at the championship, and he admits: 'Sometimes it was more stressful than racing.

'I'd go Concorde to JFK, then take my own plane down to an airfield near home in Pennsylvania. There was another strip even closer to my home town of Nazareth, but the runway wasn't really long enough, so it was a bit too character-building on a regular basis ...'

In 1970 Andretti started five Formula One races in a March, in the process logging his first finish in a championship race: a third at Spain. At South Africa in 1971, in his first time out in a Ferrari, he won his first race. He immediately followed this up by winning both heats of the non-championship Questor Grand Prix at Ontario, a Frankenstein race that pitted F1 cars against US Formula 5000 machines. The remainder of 1971 and the '72 season saw him compete in nine more races for Ferrari with only mediocre results.

Prior to 1976 one might have wagered money that, should Andretti be destined to achieve great things in Formula One, considering his background the fates would decree that it be with the Prancing Horse of Maranello. Curiously, though, this was not to be. He left Ferrari at the end of 1972, and when a two-year ride (he skipped the 1973 season to concentrate on USAC events) in the eminently forgettable Parnelli evaporated with that team early in '76, it was back to Lotus that he turned for his next Formula One opportunity. Andretti's hook-up with Colin Chapman at Long Beach was a godsend to both.

The then out-of-luck Andretti eventually got a fabulous car – the ground-effects Lotus 79 – with which to win the 1978 championship. The equally out-of-luck Chapman got a no-nonsense driver with the critical eye and gritty determination required to shake out both Team Lotus and its suspect cars.

Andretti declared the 1976 Lotus 77 to be a dog, but won a pole and race with it anyway, both at Japan. In 1977 Chapman pulled out of his magic hat the Lotus 78, the first real 'wing car'. Andretti piloted it to victory at Long Beach, and it looked so promising early in the year that people started talking championship for him and Lotus. Its season sank, however, following teething problems with a new version of the Cosworth engine.

The 78 carried Andretti and Lotus through the first five races of 1978, gaining him one victory. Zolder was the debut of the Lotus 79, the ultimate in ground effects. In an accomplishment reminiscent of the Lotus 49 at Zandvoort 11 years earlier, the 79 took pole and the win its first time out. Andretti kept it up with wins at Spain, France, Germany and Holland. So dominant was Lotus in 1978 that Andretti's major competition for the title was his team-mate, SuperSwede Ronnie Peterson.

Andretti came to Monza leading Peterson by 12 points. At the start, James Hunt was punted into Peterson by another car. Peterson's car in turn hit the Armco heavily and burst into flames. The race was red-flagged as Hunt, Patrick Depailler, Clay Regazzoni and race marshals worked bravely to free Peterson.

The accident had been frightening to witness, but Peterson was taken away to the hospital with only severely broken legs and minor burns. Andretti made the second start thinking that his team-mate was going to be OK. After chasing down Gilles Villeneuve and finishing first on the track, Andretti was relegated to sixth for jumping the restart. This was sufficient, though, under the circumstances, to clinch the championship.

At first Peterson's injuries appeared to be survivable, but the severe trauma to his legs caused blood clots to form in his circulatory system. He died the next morning. Needless to say, the tragedy doused much of Andretti's immediate enjoyment of his triumph. As he left the hospital Andretti put it simply: 'Unhappily,' he said, 'motor racing is also this ...'

Peterson's death deeply saddened Andretti. The Swedish driver was his best friend and for several weeks he struggled to come to terms with the loss. With the passage of time, however, Monza 1978, though it is certainly remembered as a dark day in Grand Prix history, is now equally well remembered as the day that Mario Andretti became only the second American to capture the world drivers' championship.

Some may argue that Andretti rode the phenomenal 79 to his championship. But it should be remembered that the 79, like most of Chapman's cars, existed just this side of the line dividing the unconquerable from the undriveable. Merely setting up a Lotus was often enough to drive strong men to distraction. Andretti joined Moss, Clark, Graham Hill, Rindt, Fittipaldi and Peterson in the select group possessing sufficient skill to bring schizophrenic Lotus machinery to near its full potential.

Andretti had won his last Formula One race. He competed for four more seasons, two with Lotus, one with Alfa Romeo, and had three races in 1982 with Williams and, once again, Ferrari. At Monza that year, his next to last Formula One race, he very authoritatively put his Ferrari on pole to the delight of the *tifosi*, among whose ranks he had once been numbered. Typical Andretti – going out with class.

At 42 Andretti was a little long in the tooth for a Formula One driver, but his racing career was far from over. For more than a decade he continued to threaten a second victory at Indy. He had the privilege of going wheel-to-wheel with his son, Michael, in Indy cars. In 1992, at the age of 52, he captured a 230 mph pole at Michigan International Speedway. Driving high performance race cars is a severe physical and psychological challenge. Just going at very high speed inflicts extreme stress on a driver's body. Many wondered how long Andretti would continue, or, for that matter, how he had continued for so long.

Andretti's Italian-American drawl and legendary coolness behind the wheel hid a fierce competitive spirit. It is possible that no other driver in the history of motor racing has had so much success while simultaneously having to put out so much effort for that success. Andretti's physical and mental makeup were perfectly suited, as perhaps no other driver's has been, to the demands of racing.

Through all those years and all those trials Andretti was never petulant, juvenile or devious, which is a great deal more than can be said for a lot of other top rank drivers in the Grand Prix pressure cooker. Sure, he could lose his temper on occasion. Making your living at 170 mph will cause that. But his behaviour was invariably a credit to his profession.

Once, at Paul Ricard, France, he went off the road at 160 mph, his car becoming airborne for some distance before crashing down to earth. 'Good flight plan, bad landing,' he said after climbing from the wreckage. Another time he talked about a new contract he had signed, and a journalist remarked that they must be paying him telephone numbers. 'Right,' he said, 'with a foreign area code …'

Despite a career that touched five decades, Andretti did not, at the end, fade away into obscurity. He would never have tolerated that. He was still winning in his fifties. At Phoenix in 1993, the year of his son's abortive try at Formula One, he took his last Indycar victory. A year earlier, I had the good fortune to meet Andretti in Texas. I wanted to ask him about his alleged habit of saying a quick prayer before each race. 'Is it true?' I asked. 'Maybe,' he replied. 'Only a fool would risk his life for a living and not have some faith in God.'

9

# Between Two Worlds

*Certain things in life can bring a person very close to the reality of how fragile life is. Motor racing is one of them. At the same moment you are doing something that nobody else is able to do. The same moment you are seen as the best, the fastest and somebody that cannot be touched, you are enormously fragile. Because in a split second it's gone.*

AYRTON SENNA

Maybe there is some truth in the theory that racing car drivers have short memories because their concept of time is different from most other people. Drivers who spend most of their waking hours combating the tiniest fraction of a second discover that time covers a multitude of sins, heals the deepest wounds, and erases the most vivid memories, if you have enough of it.

They live in a different dimension: 'between two worlds', as Ayrton Senna once remarked in response to a question about his Monte Carlo experience – the almost supernatural drive of a lifetime when the three-times world champion became 'detached' from his body during several phenomenal qualifying laps prior to the 1988 Monaco Grand Prix.

More of that later in this chapter, but first allow me to echo Senna's thoughts about the reason why, he believed, many drivers can focus on the future so easily even in the immediate aftermath of tragedy. Is it possible that these courageous, ambitiously insane racers pursue their own dreams at such breathtaking speed and intensity that the past cannot catch up with them? Remember Jim Clark's words, a few days after his close friend and team-mate Alan

Stacey died at Spa, Belgium, in 1960: 'It's difficult for the past to haunt someone who is forever hurtling into the future. In this game you don't have time to look back.'

Senna's point exactly. 'Racing drivers exist in a world that is measured in fractions of seconds but at the same time our entire lives, everything we have worked hard to become and everything we hope to be, is put on the line in the very short space of time that makes up a Grand Prix race. Decisions that could be the difference between success and failure, and life and death, are made in the blink of an eye. When you exist in this intense, surreal environment, you look at things differently and react to situations differently, you do not allow yourself to be held to ransom by emotions, especially fear.'

Senna meant what he said, but this was before his experience at Jerez de la Frontera during qualifying for the 1990 Spanish Grand Prix. What happened changed Senna for the rest of his life and he became something of a case study for the neuro-scientists who believe in the theory of fear conditioning. Senna was traumatized by the events of Friday 28 September and, possibly, never got over it, such was the shock to his system; emotionally and mentally.

It is widely accepted that trauma, whether experienced first or second hand, can lay down strong emotional memory which is strengthened by adrenaline. In the case of a racing driver who has a serious accident or, in Senna's case, is exposed to the trauma of someone else's misfortune, fear conditioning can occur.

Ayrton Senna was deeply disturbed by what he saw at Jerez and it came back to haunt him shortly before his death – intense fear triggered by the trauma of Imola 1994. It was then that Clark's theory about ghosts from the past and Senna's own belief in immunity from emotional ransom fell apart – in the punishing heat and choking dust of Jerez, Senna touched the dark side of Formula One and was never the same.

At 1.52 on the Friday qualifying session of the 1990 Spanish Grand Prix, Lotus driver Martin Donnelly struck a barrier virtually head-on at 147 mph. What remained of the car looked like something which had been savagely torn to pieces and Donnelly lay in the middle of the track. Photographs of the accident represent some of the most grotesquely dramatic images ever captured in Formula One.

Donnelly's Lotus, moments after impact, is reduced to flying debris in a cloud of dust and smoke; it looks as though a bomb has blown car and driver apart, such is the extent of the damage. Two-thirds of the car is missing, disintegrated by the ferocity of the impact, leaving a small yellow section of body on the grass by the barrier and parts of the engine, cockpit, and the wheels strewn in several different directions. Donnelly, thrown violently through the air and on to the tarmac, is a twisted, motionless piece of human debris; he looks like a crash dummy, ejected like a bullet from the wreckage.

The Spanish television camera remained on him a long time, lingering there for what seemed like an unbearable age, although in truth it was no more than a couple of minutes. This is the amount of time it took race doctor Professor Sid Watkins to reach the scene. He, like everyone else at Jerez, thought that Donnelly could not have survived such a violent accident.

'There was a lot of debris around but the urgent thing was to get Donnelly's crash helmet open and then off,' Watkins recalled. 'On opening the visor I could see his face was blue with lack of oxygen so we sucked out his airway through his nose and connected an oxygen flow. We cut the helmet strap and slid the helmet off. Donnelly was completely unconscious. His teeth were tightly clenched and I had to force his jaws apart with an artery clamp to get an airway in so we could suck out secretions and blood from the pharynx and nose, and get a good flow of oxygen into him. He had bad fractures in the legs and there was a lot of swelling and blood loss in the fracture sites. But remarkably after 20 minutes he started to speak. He was in a bad way, especially his legs, but he was alive and considering the size of the accident, that was a miracle.'

Senna was told of Donnelly and he was close to tears. He walked to where Donnelly still lay and remained there a long time. He was not required to go, no protocol demanded that he go; but he went, and he stood, and he returned to the motorhome and he asked everyone else to leave. 'I wanted to be alone with my thoughts. They were private moments and I doubt that I will ever be able to express what I felt.'

In his biography of Senna, *The Hard Edge of Genius*, Christopher Hilton wrote: 'Why did Senna go to where Donnelly lay? In part because, I believe, his religious convictions took him there to face it, in part because he was now becoming a seignor in Grand Prix racing, very possibly a potential spokesman for safety and he felt he should have been there; in part because he cared very deeply about the consequence of human actions.'

On the evening of Friday 28 September, Senna visited Donnelly at the Polytrauma Hospital in Seville. As well as smashing both legs, Donnelly had suffered bruising of the left side of his brain and of the lungs. But he recognized Senna and the Brazilian was again moved to tears. He felt deep compassion for Donnelly but also a strange gnawing deep in his own soul; the torment of fear. Subconsciously, Senna now believed he would one day end up like Donnelly, or worse. Maybe when his time came he would not cheat death.

It is possible that the sight of Donnelly on the track at Jerez and in the hospital bed at Seville altered Senna's risk perception. Before he thought he was invulnerable, expecting accidents to happen to other drivers and not himself. In his own mind Senna believed he was less likely than the average driver to suffer the bad things in Formula One and more likely than the average driver to experience the good things. Senna believed he was less likely than the average driver to have an accident because he was more skilful. But Donnelly's fate made Senna feel vulnerable.

The incident at Jerez haunted Senna for a long time, possibly until the end of his life. The foreboding presence of intrusive thoughts, dark memories of Donnelly's twisted body and flashes of the horror of the violent destruction of the Lotus, were often accompanied by deep distress; symptoms of post-traumatic stress disorder. Senna suffered in silence.

But why Donnelly's accident? It was not the first time Senna had seen motor racing wreak havoc on machine and man. During his Formula One career, from March 1984 to Jerez 1990, and beyond to May 1994 – the end of his life – Senna witnessed many terrible accidents and he rarely gave them a second thought, even though the catalogue of death and serious injury between his first and last Formula One race is the stuff of nightmares:

1984: Martin Brundle broke his legs in Dallas, Texas; Johnny Cecotto had very severe leg injuries at Brands Hatch, England; Piercarlo Ghinzani crashed and received burns at Kyalami, South Africa; Patrick Tambay fractured his leg in an accident at Monte Carlo, Monaco.

1986: Elio de Angelis suffered brain damage and died after a shocking accident testing a Brabham at Paul Ricard, France; Jacques Laffite had an accident at Brands Hatch, severely injuring his legs and pelvis and ending his Formula One career.

1989:  Philippe Streiff crashed at Rio, Brazil, in unofficial practice, injuring his neck and, tragically, developing spinal cord complications which left him tetraplegic.
1992:  Christian Fittipaldi broke his neck at Magny Cours, France.

Senna witnessed most of these and many more accidents, most of which could have proved fatal to the drivers involved, but it wasn't until Donnelly almost died at Jerez that something inside Senna snapped. He'd seen enough and in those few moments of deep reflection, as he pondered Donnelly's fate and searched his soul for answers to the questions he was now asking, Senna came to a shocking conclusion: 'I am afraid of death.'

How could this happen to a man who only a year before had been accused of possessing the risk perception of someone who believed they were completely invulnerable? Senna drove as though he was invincible, somehow protected by a power greater than himself.

On Sunday 21 October 1990, at the Suzuka circuit in Japan, Senna certainly drove like a man who was not afraid to die. Senna was world champion, unless Alain Prost could beat him across the full 53 laps, the full 192.953 miles of the Grand Prix, to prevent it, and perhaps become champion himself in the final race at Adelaide.

But Prost never stood a chance. He was up against a man whose mind had reached beyond the realms of human nature. A strong spirit of immortality possessed Senna and if it came to it, he would not hesitate to put his, or anyone else's, life on the line. And that is what happened at Suzuka; 16 seconds of Senna madness that threatened to kill him and Prost.

Senna had pole position in his Marlboro McLaren Honda but less than two seconds into the Japanese Grand Prix, Prost had nosed his way ahead. At six seconds Prost was completely in front, Senna directly behind him. At seven seconds Prost had his Ferrari positioned mid-track, hurtling into the first corner: an unfolding right. At eight seconds Senna had thrust his McLaren towards the inside of Prost. At nine seconds Senna's front wheels were alongside the flank of the Ferrari. Prost was still turning into the corner, still turning across Senna.

What was Senna thinking? That he was a ghost rider in a phantom car? That he could defy the laws of physics and just shoot past Prost as if he wasn't really there? Was Senna the only one who didn't cringe at the insanity of his actions?

At 10 seconds they touched. Everyone watching knew they would, Prost knew it, and so did Senna. The Ferrari's rear wing was torn off and thrown violently away like debris on to the track, the McLaren's front left wheel was wrenched off and both cars, out of control and locked together in a savage embrace, left the track and ploughed across the run-off area. At 16 seconds they smashed into the tyre-wall, sending a tremor through it. The two cars, or what was left of them, were separated by the impact; a few feet apart and engulfed in dust. Incredibly, both drivers were unhurt.

'He did it on purpose,' Prost would say. 'He pushed me off to win the championship.' The Frenchman was badly shaken, not by the crash, but by Senna's 'insanity'. 'I'm not ready to fight against irresponsible people on the track who are not afraid to die,' he added. 'Senna has a problem. He thinks he can't kill himself because he believes in God and I think that's very dangerous for the other drivers.'

Senna denied the allegation, but Prost had a point. There was some truth in what he said after the incident at Suzuka, because since he had 'renewed' his faith in God, in the summer of 1988, Senna's risk perception had altered. Risks he would never have taken before were suddenly being wildly embraced; the greater the danger, the higher the stakes, the more Senna went for it. 'It's much worse than a death wish,' Prost remarked, 'Senna thinks he's indestructible!'

Raised a Catholic, Senna always had a faith in God but it wasn't until the 28th year of his life that this faith 'came to life' – 1988, his first world title, and Senna recalls: 'I had a highly special experience and felt God's presence very strongly. On the day I became world champion – Sunday 30th October at Suzuka, Japan – I had the feeling that I was with Him and that He was with me. It has been like this since Monte Carlo.'

Monte Carlo had been five months earlier: after the Monaco Grand Prix, Senna searched his soul following an accident as he was leading on lap 67 of the tight road circuit. It was Sunday 15 May, early evening, a few hours after Senna lost concentration just before the tunnel and crashed badly. He was unhurt but shaken and worried that the crash could cost him the championship. He spent an hour praying, asking God for help.

'It was the turning point of the 1988 season,' he recalled some years later. 'It was nothing to do with the car or the equipment. The mistake I made could have ended in disaster and it changed me psychologically and mentally. I changed a lot inside. It gave me the strength and power to fight in critical moments. It was the biggest step in my career as a professional, a racing driver and a man.

'It brought me closer to God than I have ever been. I was feeling easy in front. It was a hundred per cent perfect weekend. Suddenly I lost concentration, made a stupid mistake and threw everything away. It could have cost me my life. It made me reflect about a lot of things, especially my relationship with God.'

Senna possessed a burning desire to transcend ordinary life, that is why he pushed himself so hard to become a Formula One driver. He would never have been satisfied with a so-called 'ordinary' existence, even though part of him was forever humble, down-to-earth. These are the two sides of Ayrton Senna.

He would say: 'If I ever happen to have an accident that eventually costs me my life, I hope it is in one go. I would not like to be in a wheelchair. I would not like to be in a hospital suffering from whatever injury it was. If I am going to live, I want to live fully. Very intensely, because I am an intense person. It would ruin my life if I had to live partially.

'As long as my passion for my profession is kept alive, my dream will be to survive. The day when this passion starts weakening, my dream will end. The Formula One is a world of strong emotions and egos where the weak don't survive.'

There are those within the close Senna family who believe Senna's passion for motor racing was weakening during the last year or two of his life. There are others who say his faith in God had become more important to him than the sport that, in the eyes of the people of Brazil, made him a god.

Fame did not change Senna. He always remained the same person, a humble and sincere friend to those he left behind living their ordinary lives, while he enjoyed the existence of a superstar. Even when he was already a three-times world champion, if he was in his home country and saw his friends eating at a roadside cafe he would park his car and stroll over to nibble from their plates, the way he always had. 'He was eager to join in, be one of us,' his friends would say. 'He had no bodyguards and made no display of being a celebrity. Part of him wanted to be normal, but part of him did not.'

Senna had a philosophical conflict but motor racing and speed were in his blood and he was always striving to achieve his goal, which was to win. He admitted to being 'obsessed' but in his defence he would claim: 'If I am obsessive it is in a positive way. I have a strong natural push but it is not unhealthy, not a disease.'

He would always try to beat other people's achievements but on so many occasions he found it was better to beat his own achievements. That often gave him more satisfaction, mainly because he did not feel happy if he was comfortable. 'Something inside me pushes me when I get comfortable. It makes me go further and want to keep pushing.

'I have to establish for myself my own limits. When I have reached those limits I want to beat them and establish new ones. I have an understanding of what I am doing, but no control over the thing inside me that pushes me. It is something I was born with, a God-given desire.' This 'natural push' gave Senna the impetus needed to scale the heights of motor racing in spectacular fashion.

He was born in São Paulo, Brazil, in 1960. He was born to race. His father first sponsored him in kart racing as a child, where he won his first go-kart championship at the age of 14, and he went on to claim two South American titles. He then moved to England to begin an apprenticeship in top-flight racing. His Brazilian fans cheered him through while he took the titles from 1981 to 1983 in progressively more powerful cars.

He first grabbed the headlines in Formula One with a dramatic drive in the wet at Monaco, placing him second behind Alain Prost in a race that was shortened because of the terrible conditions. The following year he was snapped up to drive for Lotus-Renault. Again driving in the wet, he won his first Grand Prix in Portugal.

From 1985 to 1987 he won six races for Lotus. In 1987 Lotus ran Honda engines, and when Honda switched in 1988 to the McLaren team Senna went with them. This led to an era of dominance of Formula One for McLaren-Honda and Senna.

In 1988 he won eight races, an all-time record, and in 1989 he won a further six races but was edged out of the championship by fellow McLaren driver Alain Prost. In 1989 he came second again to Prost, but only due to his exclusion from the Japanese Grand Prix. The next two consecutive years he won the crown, in 1990 winning six races for McLaren-Honda, and in 1991 seven.

He competed in 161 Grand Prix races and won 41 of them. He was the Formula One champion in 1988, 1990 and 1991. He was a god to the Brazilians, maybe even more so than the great Pele. But unlike Pele, Senna had a fatal flaw. He could not stop pushing. He could not let go. He could not live life anywhere else except at the limit.

Senna became an emotion junkie. He had to feel alive, in the extreme sense of the word. In 1989, a few months after winning his first world championship, he admitted: 'I need to experience emotion in its most heightened, intense form. We are all made of emotions. We are all looking for emotions. It's just a question of finding a way to experience them.

'One thing Formula One can provide you with is real emotion because you are always exposed to danger, of getting hurt, of dying.'

Until Imola, 1 May 1994, Senna had never been present at a race meeting where a driver died, but he'd been in several crashes of his own – notably in Mexico and at Hockenheim – which might have been very bad; and he'd been present at race meetings where crashes could have been fatal: in addition to those mentioned previously, in particular Martin Donnelly's horrific accident at Jerez in 1990, there had been Gerhard Berger at Imola in 1989, Derek Warwick at Monza and Riccardo Patrese at Estoril in 1992, Christian Fittipaldi at Monza and Alessandro Zanardi at Spa in 1993.

When Zanardi's Lotus broke out of control, spewing debris and wreckage everywhere, Senna came upon the scene at 160 mph and had to throw his car sideways to avoid the safety marshals. It was after that near miss that he became angry at certain sections of the media who put his escape down to the assumption that 'someone up there must be looking out for Ayrton Senna'. He knew it was true. After all, his faith in God was by now more important to him than motor racing itself, only Senna did not want people to believe that he was no longer in control of his own destiny.

# 10

# When the Soul Departs

*My relationship with God is more important to me than anything else in my life.*

AYRTON SENNA, 1993

Ayrton Senna never felt it necessary to confront those who felt his faith in God led him to believe that God would protect him. They were simply talking nonsense. It went without saying that he suffered no such delusions – or so he made out – and it is hard to accept that anyone of Senna's intelligence and perception could think otherwise, although no one ever really knew what he was thinking.

There did come a time in his life, probably in the weeks and months after he 'renewed his faith in God' in 1988, when Senna began to pray before races, asking God to help him to focus, to perform at a higher level, exist for two hours on a different plane; that place between two worlds.

His infamous ride at Monte Carlo during practice for the 1988 Monaco Grand Prix, paints a vivid picture of the point Senna had reached in his career and life; he had transcended natural human existence to occupy a place on the extreme rim of consciousness.

On the last qualifying session Senna was already on pole and was going faster and faster. 'One lap after the other, quicker and quicker and quicker,' he said. 'I was at one stage just on pole, then by half a second and then one second and I kept going. Suddenly I was nearly two seconds faster than anybody else, including my team-mate with the same car. And I suddenly realized I was no longer driving the car consciously.

'I was kind of driving it by instinct, only I was in a different dimension. It was like I was in a tunnel. Not only the tunnel under the hotel but the whole circuit was a tunnel. I was just going and going, more and more and more and more. I was way over the limit but still able to find even more. Then suddenly something just kicked me. I kind of woke up and realized that I was in a different atmosphere than you normally are. My immediate reaction was to back off, slow down.

'I drove back slowly to the pits and didn't want to go out any more that day. It frightened me because I realized I was well beyond my conscious understanding.'

Although Senna did not refer to what happened at Monte Carlo as being a religious experience, it was in no way purely subliminal. Two days later Senna would admit: 'I was very aware of God's presence, there was certainly a higher power at work as well as some kind of controlling force below the threshold of consciousness.'

Of his beliefs, he'd say in a 1993 interview: 'Thanks to God I have a deep faith in God and in Jesus Christ. My life changed greatly as soon as I experienced that faith. The strength that emanates from God where I myself am concerned, I feel that I have enjoyed a great privilege. He has given me lots of strength when times were the hardest, and lots of joy in the happiest moments.

'In this godless world there are lots of people looking for religion. They are desperate for it. I am only being truthful. I am saying what I believe and what I feel. You offer religion to those who want it.'

Senna never made a big deal about his faith, but on occasions he could say words to make an atheist squirm, and at other times fire four-letter words at the press or lunge at fellow drivers. He was something of a paradox; not often understood, never predictable, always seeking the inconceivable. One thing is certain, though, on 1 May 1994 he needed God more than ever before. On that day Senna was broken inside, and he never had the chance to mend.

The image of the twisted, smoking metal and scattered debris of Roland Ratzenberger's wrecked Simtek-Ford car, at the apex of Imola's Tosa bend, was too much for Senna to take in. For a moment he could not believe what he was seeing, even though he had seen it all before. There was something surreal about the whole thing even though it was the harshest reality he had ever faced. Painful memories of Jerez came flooding back and with them the pain of human suffering. He felt deep compassion for Ratzenberger and also fear; this terrible image of a man close to death frightened Senna, but his own feeling of vulnerability frightened him even more. At that precise moment, as the overhead TV screens in the Williams garage provided a chilling view of the dying Ratzenberger, Senna knew he could not take part in the Italian Grand Prix. The still small voice inside him said: 'Walk away, while you can.'

Williams-Renault engineer Bernard Dudot recalls: 'Ayrton was right behind us in the garage and he witnessed everything on the monitors when Ratzenberger was killed in his fatal accident. Now he had learned first hand about death. I saw him encountering that experience not just as an onlooker but as a concerned human being.'

As the awful scene unfolded and doctors attended to Ratzenberger, performing intravenous infusion, intubation, ventilation and cardiopulmonary resuscitation in a desperate attempt to save the stricken driver's life, Senna found himself rooted to the spot, unable to turn his eyes away from the screen. He watched for a short while, observing the incident, trying to mask his own fear, then turned away, removed his ear plugs and closed his eyes for a moment, trying to compose himself. He had another quick glance at the monitor above him. His eyes misted, tears formed. He took a deep breath and sighed, closed his eyes again for a moment, and then left the room. He wasn't sure where he was going, yet, but he had to do something.

'He was supposed to get back into his car,' Dudot added. 'But, as I watched, he became pale and haggard, and was obviously unable to hoist himself into the driver's seat. I felt deeply sorry for him, and worried. It had affected him very seriously. He was stricken in the deepest recesses of his being.'

In *Life at the Limit* track doctor Professor Sid Watkins remembers Senna suddenly appearing at the door of the Imola medical centre minutes after Ratzenberger had been airlifted by helicopter to the Maggiore Hospital in Bologna. Watkins wrote:

> *[Senna] had been to the scene of the accident in a course car that he had commandeered (for which he was later chastised) and, having questioned the marshals about the accident, went to the medical centre area, where he had been debarred from entering.*
>
> *But he had jumped over the fence at the rear to get to the door of the unit. I took him round to the circuit side of the area and answered*

*his questions with complete honesty. As we talked, Charlie Moody, the team manager of Simtek, arrived. I then had to tell him the bad news that Ratzenberger was beyond medical help.*

Senna was beside himself. He broke down and cried on Watkins' shoulder. He could not cope any more. His soul was so full of pain it felt as though he was being torn apart. So much grief, so much fear and he began to sob.

It was obvious to Watkins that Senna was in no fit state to take part in the race so he said: 'Ayrton, why don't you withdraw from racing tomorrow? I don't think you should do it. In fact, why won't you give it up altogether? What else do you need to do? You have been world champion three times, you are obviously the quickest driver. Give it up.'

Senna was silent. Watkins continued. 'I don't think the risk is worth continuing – pack it in!' Senna composed himself, gave Watkins a very steady look and, now calm, said: 'Sid, there are certain things over which we have no control. I cannot quit, I have to go on.'

That night, after sharing a meal with some Brazilian friends and having a chat with team manager Frank Williams, Senna prayed. He prayed for an hour or more and felt much better. Deep inside he still felt troubled, as though he really should quit, but he had asked God to keep him safe during the Italian Grand Prix, because afterwards, or at least at the end of the season, he would seriously think about retiring. Part of him wanted out, but for now he had obligations to fulfil, and of course he had no control of his desire to win at Imola, despite his fear of ending up like Ratzenberger. In a phone call to his girlfriend before he went to bed, he indicated that he did not want to race the next day, but had to because it was his job.

The weekend at Imola had not been pleasant for anybody, but Senna had been affected more than most. It seemed as though he had taken the whole weight of responsibility for this awful 48 hours of motor racing hell on his shoulders and was slowly being crushed by it. His mind kept going back to the first day of practice when Rubens Barrichello, driving for the Jordan team, hit a kerb in a chicane and launched his vehicle over a tyre barrier straight into a debris fence. While the crash looked horrific, he escaped with a broken nose and some other minor injuries.

Senna spent an hour or more with Barrichello before Ratzenberger died. He wanted to hear Barrichello's version of events, to get it clear in his own mind who or what was responsible for the accident. Senna had plans to try to re-form the Drivers' Association to give Formula One drivers more power to force safety changes. He was very concerned about the issue of safety in racing, and the death of Ratzenberger brought the danger of his sport very close to him. Nobody had died in Formula One while Senna was racing in it, which may have allowed him to put his own mortality to the back of his mind. But suddenly his mortality was staring him right in the face, along with the terrifying image of Ratzenberger's awful fate.

On the morning of the race Senna put on a brave face. He had not slept well. Nightmares had disturbed him, but he was determined to go through with it, and win. He had prayed again and believed God would look after him. He sat quietly in the Williams garage next to his car waiting for the call to go to the starting grid. When the time came Senna had the look of a man about to face his own execution. Someone had to tap him on the arm to get his attention, such was Senna's deeply troubled state of mind. He breathed deeply, held his breath for a moment, closed his eyes and let out a sigh. He didn't want to race.

Out on the grid, while the vibrant Grand Prix circus boomed and crashed around his ears, Senna sat quietly in the cockpit of his car. He was there in person but not in spirit. He had a solemn look about him, you could see it in his eyes before he closed them and prayed silently. The last words he said before he put on his helmet were: 'Okay, everything's fine.' He was lying.

Ominously, the race had to run its first few laps behind a safety pace car due to an incident on the starting grid. The Lotus driven by Pedro Lamy had slammed into the rear of J. J. Lehto's Benetton, which had stalled on the grid. Debris flew on to the crowd, over the debris fence and injured nine spectators.

As the race restarted from behind the pace car, Senna and Michael Schumacher drove away from the rest of the field. As the pair drove into the Tamburello curve, a flat-out long left hand turn, for the first time after the start, Schumacher saw the bottom of Senna's car hit the road due to bumps on the track. He also stated later in court that Senna's car had seemed very unstable in that corner. The very next lap, Senna lost control of the car at 190 mph, jumping the kerb and slamming into an unprotected concrete wall at an acute angle.

Senna had managed to slow the car to 130 mph just before the impact, but even with the strength of the cars this was not enough, although the safety cell in the car remained largely intact. The front suspension collapsed and the front wheel and part of the suspension came around the side of the cockpit striking Senna in the head, the massive head injuries killing him. Medical emergency crews were on the scene within a minute and did everything possible to give the driver the best chance of survival. Even with this attention, Senna was pronounced brain dead before the end of the race.

Officially he died in hospital late that afternoon. Actually Senna died at the wall.

The reason for Senna's death has never been finalized. A court case and intensive investigation failed to highlight any one over-riding contributing factor for which blame could be laid. Frank Williams and two of his engineers faced manslaughter charges, as did two track employees, but nothing could be proved and the charges were dropped – luckily, for the sport, avoiding the setting of a dangerous precedent.

Many factors appear to have militated against Senna surviving the accident, the track especially. Tamburello corner was notoriously rough, a factor Senna himself had sought to remedy during pre-season testing at the track. There had been some resurfacing in places, although some say that the surface actually became worse with bumps up to 5cm high in places. Formula One cars cannot handle bumps like that for very long without sustaining damage. The suspension systems are very firm and only allow small amounts of wheel travel, a situation which would have reduced the amount of friction of the tyres with the road while traversing rough surfaces.

It is possible that there was a suspension failure due to the bumps, causing the car to veer off. This has not been proven either way, as the car was so badly damaged upon impact as to make positive conclusions impossible to draw.

The steering column in Senna's car had snapped and was found outside the vehicle after the impact. This column had been cut and welded together again at the driver's request for more room in the cockpit. The prosecution in the Senna manslaughter court case tried to prove that the column had broken prior to the impact, causing the loss of control. This also was never proven, the Williams engineers saying that it broke as a result of the crash, although they did concede that it may have been partially cracked before impact.

Another avoidable factor in the death of Senna was the design of the track at that point. As well as being bumpy, there was a stream very close to the track. Either this stream should have been redirected or the track design should have taken it into account. As it was, neither of these two options was followed. The result was a need to stop cars before they went into the stream. A corner like this should have a runoff area provided, to allow time for the cars to regain control or to reduce their speed before impact. There was no room in this case between the track and the concrete barrier for any runoff. A sand trap was considered, but yet again, there was insufficient room for it to be built.

Tyres were considered but never used due to their proximity to the track. For tyres to be effective at speed, a wall at least three tyres deep is required, which would have come very close to the racing surface. This is undesirable as even a slightly wayward car may be caught by the tyres and thus be unable to continue. The only option available to race organizers without incurring major reconstruction costs was a concrete runoff area, giving traction to sliding cars, which might be able to regain control. This still left a horribly unprotected, unforgiving concrete wall on the outside of a very high-speed corner, although Senna was able to use the concrete area to slow his vehicle a little. Tamburello curve has since been realigned to bring the cars away from the wall earlier, and better barriers now protect errant vehicles.

Another possible factor in the cause of the accident was the presence of a small foreign object on the track surface, seen in front of Senna supposedly just before the entrance to the fatal corner. It has been suggested that the object may have caused mechanical damage as Senna drove over it, but again there is no evidence that any damage it may have caused played a part in Senna's loss of control. The television footage of the object on the track was later analysed and it was found that the object was actually 700 metres from where Senna left the circuit.

The 'black box' data recorder in the vehicle was unable to provide any information about the accident. Not only did it disappear for about a month before it could be examined; when it resurfaced, it was smashed beyond repair, possibly with a hammer. Also missing was the last 1.7 seconds of video from Senna's on-board camera. This has never been recovered, but may well hold the secret to what really happened on that tragic day.

Telemetry sent into the Williams pits from Senna's car shows Senna lifted off the power slightly just before he left the track. It has been speculated that when the car jumped over the bumps on the track on the previous lap, the partly cracked steering column may have flexed as the car skipped across the bumps. This would have unsettled the car the way Schumacher described in court. The next time he approached the corner, Senna was naturally cautious and lifted off slightly, an action which, combined with the rough surface, may have caused the loss of traction that sent the car off the track. This argument makes sense, but it was discounted by the prosecution who accused the Williams technicians of falsifying the telemetry readings.

Regardless of the actual cause of the accident, Senna's death has brought a great deal of change into the regulations of Formula One. Many of these regulations were not implemented until the beginning of the 1998 season after extensive research by the sport's governing body, the FIA (see pp. 171–83). Tracks have been made safer and more forgiving, the cars both safer and slower, although some of the new regulations are seen as dangerous by some drivers. The design of the cockpit now offers far more protection to the driver's head as well as being twice as strong as previous years. Side impact protection has been improved and teams must show that an effort has been made to reduce the chance of a wayward front wheel hitting the driver in the event of an accident. The very next year, the engine size was decreased from 3.5 litres to 3 litres to reduce the speed of the vehicles, an engine configuration which remains today.

In fact, 1994 was the first year of racing after controversial computer-controlled technologies were banned. One such technology was 'active suspension', which constantly sensed the needs of the car and adjusted the spring and damper rates accordingly for maximum traction. Another banned technology was traction control, which reduced the power to the driving wheels on loss of traction, giving the driver a far greater chance of recovering a loss of control. These technologies made the cars safer at speed, but also faster. They were banned after consideration of both speed-limiting and cost factors, the smaller teams being unable to afford the high development costs. Any computer controlling of the race car was also banned, the idea being to bring the racing back to the driver instead of the car. This ruling banned the practice of adjusting the tuning of the car's engine management system and suspension from the pits, based on real-time information being sent back from the cars themselves.

It has been calculated that if the Formula One cars had not been restricted in development from 1980, they would currently be lapping Britain's Silverstone course about 20 seconds per lap faster. Theoretical average speeds would be about 200 mph instead of 140 mph, and top speeds would be around 300 mph instead of the current 180 mph. These theoretical cars would be virtually impossible to drive physically at the limit and the races would be dependent on the physical stamina of the drivers, a situation best avoided.

As for the death of Ayrton Senna, the only person who really knows what happened that day died in the accident. The truth may never be known and while it was a tragedy, the sport has become significantly safer because of his death. He would have wanted it that way and maybe, just maybe, it was his destiny.

It seems fitting, therefore, to close this chapter with the words of Professor Sid Watkins, the man who tried to save Senna's life moments after the accident at Tamburello. 'He looked serene,' Watkins recalled. 'I raised his eyelids and it was clear from his pupils that he had a massive brain injury. We lifted him from the cockpit and laid him on the ground. As we did he sighed and I felt his soul departed at that moment.'

# 11

# Reality Check

*When the end comes I hope it's spectacular. I would rather check out of this life at high speed than in my sleep. No guts no glory, that's what motor racing is all about.*

RONNIE PETERSON, SIX MONTHS BEFORE HIS DEATH AT MONZA

The lucky escape of British driver Mark Blundell in 1996 in Brazil was considered by many who witnessed it to be a miracle. While travelling at around 200 mph, the brakes failed on his Pac-West Reynard Indy car on lap 10 of the race, putting him into the concrete wall without slowing down at all.

Blundell should have died, or at least been crippled. The fact that he walked away from the accident, or hobbled to be more precise, is beyond belief. The fact that the experience increased his appetite for the danger of motor sport is even more incredible and, to a certain extent, proves the theory of Ronnie Peterson.

Peterson, the Swedish driver who died at Monza in 1978, reckoned that for every driver unnerved by a crash or near miss, nine others are 'fired-up' by the experience and push themselves and their cars to greater limits afterwards. 'It's a strange phenomenon, but true,' Peterson said, 'especially if you escape from a bad accident without getting seriously hurt. It makes you feel invincible and gives you a greater desire to go out there and do it again. It's pretty rare that an accident has a negative effect on a driver. It's usually just the opposite.'

Asked whether 'a brush with death' could result in a religious or quasi-religious experience for the driver involved, Peterson paused for a long time before answering. The concept touched a chord of truth in his soul. 'I can't speak for anyone else, but for me the answer is maybe, in certain circumstances.

'There have been one or two times, during an accident, when I've said a quick prayer. It's a natural reaction, even if you don't believe in God. And strangely, even though accidents in this sport happen so quickly, you do have time to think. It's amazing really, but sometimes, during a crash, everything kind of goes in slow motion. You have time to think that you might die, you are aware of what is happening, and yes, in my case, sometimes you think about God. But mostly racing car drivers are a cynical bunch. We have little time for religion. It has no place in motor racing.

'Most drivers facing the impact of a crash would probably think "Oh shit, this is it," and face it in a rather unemotional kind of way. It's the way we are; very analytical, clinical and pragmatic.'

Mark Blundell is a case in point. During what should have been the last moments of his life, he did not spare a thought for God or any other aspect of life after death, resorting instead to damage limitation mode and calmly accepting the fact that he was probably going to die. His experience is not unique but the way he reacted during and afterwards provides a poignant insight into the mind of a racing driver.

Brake failure, along with fire, is a driver's worst nightmare, although it left Blundell, 29 at the time, with just a broken foot in Rio de Janeiro. He was competing in his second Indycar race after switching from Formula One on a track considered to be one of the roughest and most treacherous circuits in the Indy calendar.

The point where the brakes failed was at the entrance to a relatively slow corner, from one of the fastest points on the circuit. The cars need to take off 90 to 95 mph before entering the corner. Had Blundell felt the brakes going before the corner, he would have stayed high on the track and merely slid around the wall. However, he had no warning that his brakes had failed and he had pulled out from the wall as he entered the braking area.

When the brake pedal went to the floor with absolutely no effect, Blundell had a split second to decide how to take off some speed before the inevitable impact. The only option was to hit his teammate, Mauricio Gugelmin, who had already slowed for the corner. He aimed his car at Gugelmin, but missed.

He tried to spin the car, but was carrying to much speed for the front wheels to grip. Blundell hit the wall at around 170 mph, at quite a high angle. The black box recorder in the car was analysed after the accident and measured a peak deceleration of just over 10G. As he sat in the car, helpless, as the concrete wall approached, Blundell thought his time had come. 'I took my arms back, off the wheel, and folded them across my chest. I tucked myself down. I said to myself, "I am not coming away from this, I am not coming away from this."

'I was so aware of what was going on. The speed: I just could not believe that I would walk away. It was me and that concrete wall. I knew I was not getting out of this one ..."This is it", no other thoughts came.'

The impact came and went, the car came to rest and Blundell started to get light-headed. He thought he was dying but refused to let it happen. He undid the seatbelt, stood up and climbed out of the wreckage. As he began to walk across the track, all of a sudden the pain of his shattered ankle reached his brain and he collapsed on the track, struggling to breathe from his badly bruised lungs. He then realized he was still alive.

The CART (Championship Automobile Racing Teams) safety team is acknowledged as one of the best in the world, consisting of 29 professional staff and six specialist vehicles that follow every race of the CART series. Three custom-made fast response vehicles, a supply vehicle, a pickup fitted with a Lear jet engine to blow the track clean and dry, and a $1 million mobile trauma and physical therapy unit on a semi-trailer, ensure the best possible chances for injured drivers. All the drivers' medical records are kept in the medical centre to be instantly available wherever the race may be.

As the CART safety crew was taking him to the medical centre, his only thoughts were to tell his wife he was OK, and to tell his team-mate that his brakes had failed. Blundell put the accident down 'as one hell of a reality check'. People who had been in the sport 15 or 20 years could not believe that he had survived the accident, let alone walked out of the wreck unaided.

The car disintegrated on impact with the wall, absorbing energy as it went. The speed of impact was substantially higher than that which killed Ayrton Senna, but the angle of impact was slighter. The front wheel and suspension came around the side of the cockpit and punctured the fuel cell; the cockpit, already quite small, was two inches narrower than it should have been. The seatbelts, which were of world standard, had stretched four or five inches, a factor which would have reduced the peak deceleration on his body, although it would have exposed him to the risk of head injury on the front of the cockpit.

The engine separated from the chassis and continued along the track, an unavoidable hazard which leaves the car with less energy to dissipate, resulting in faster deceleration for the safety cell containing the driver, and thus subjecting him to even higher forces. This is, however, more desirable than the engine crushing the safety cell from behind. The chassis coped surprisingly well during the impact.

Recent safety regulations had increased the strength of the safety cells that contained the drivers, especially the front section of the cockpit, making the cockpit both roomier and stronger. A lot of work had been done to strengthen the front of Indy cars since the accident in 1995 on the first lap of the Indy 500, where American driver Stan Fox was left hanging off the front of his destroyed car. A new 'energy management device' to support the head and neck under massive force had also been introduced to the cars that very year. All of the above factors worked together in some way to save Mark Blundell.

In 1997 and 1998, Blundell used a special seat, as required by new regulations introduced in 1997. It meets all the requirements for padding alongside the driver's torso. It is made from kevlar and lined with compressed polystyrene and trimmed with fireproof Nomex. The lining of the seat was almost identical to the lining of a standard crash helmet, protecting and supporting Blundell's back. This seat saved him from back injuries in a practice accident in 1997 when he slammed the concrete wall backwards at 140 mph.

Blundell, while considering himself 'damn lucky to be alive', remains rather passive about the whole experience. 'It didn't change my life in any way,' he said, 'and it did not take me long to get over it. I was soon racing again and my desire to keep pushing for success was in no way diminished. In fact, the accident probably gave me a greater desire to continue in the sport. Most drivers would probably feel the same way. We are a strange breed of people.'

## 12

# The Joker

*There are only two reasons why a racing driver's career should end; common sense or death. The latter is obviously the least preferable but unfortunately the most common.*

JUAN MANUEL FANGIO

There is certainly nothing strange about Gerhard Berger, not even the fact that he risked his life for fun and not fame or fortune. The Austrian driver, despite his 'good-time' approach to the world's most dangerous sport, is just about as normal as you can get in an otherwise uncertain climate of eccentricity and other unorthodox behaviour.

This is the man of whom McLaren chief Ron Dennis once said: 'Of all the drivers I have known, Gerhard is the one who would drive for nothing. He has always been in love with motor racing.'

Humour and a laid-back philosophy of life and death have been Berger's constant currency, even though the usual medium of exchange in Formula One is a sobering mixture of blood, sweat, tears and a few nervous breakdowns. Berger is different. He's the joker in a pack of serious-looking racing aces and speed kings, although he has rarely been dealt a decent hand and, on more than one occasion, has held the death card in his palm, as is the case with most Grand Prix drivers.

In November 1995 Berger escaped unhurt from a 100 mph testing accident driving for Benetton-Renault at Estoril in Portugal. The Austrian, having his first run in the Benetton since leaving Ferrari, lost control on the entry to the high-speed Parabolica corner and slammed hard into a wall, damaging the B195 beyond repair. 'I was going for a quick time and I just lost it,' said Berger. He was lucky.

The following month Berger crashed his new Benetton Formula One car three times in three weeks; two 100 mph shunts at Estoril in Portugal and a particularly dramatic spin into the barriers at Barcelona's 150 mph Curvone Renault corner threatened to end his career if not his life. But once again fortune favoured the lucky Austrian.

He broke his neck in a road car accident at the end of 1984, and could have died when his Ferrari went straight off at Tamburello during the 1989 San Marino Grand Prix. He fractured ribs and suffered burns after fuel soaked into his uniform but it was a miracle he survived at all. Two big accidents driving for Ferrari at Interlagos in 1993, one in practice and the other at the first corner at the start of the race, when Michael Andretti took him off, could also have ended his life. Berger simply took it all in his stride. No fuss, just a stiff drink to calm the nerves.

As he looked ahead to retirement in the autumn of 1997, Berger, forever the comedian, said he might just join the Japanese driver Ukyo Katayama, who was also leaving the sport, to take up the challenge of mountaineering. 'I think I will climb Everest with him,' said Berger, 'just as long as there is a nice bar at the top.'

He was kidding around, but knocking back a stiff drink while hanging on to the roof of the world is just the kind of crazy stunt Berger would have enjoyed before time overtook him at the age of 38, displaying a rear plate that said: *'Don't tempt fate!'*

Figuratively speaking of course, but after 14 seasons, 10 wins, 45 podium appearances and races in the colours of Benetton, Ferrari, Arrows and McLaren, Berger knew that it was time to go. Just a trace of sadness filled his eternally smiling eyes as he prepared to climb into a Grand Prix car for the 210th and last race of his brilliant career at Jerez. But his decision to retire after the 1997 European Grand Prix in Spain was met with a mixture of regret and relief.

Regret because his departure would rob Formula One of a character more closely identified with the colourful image of a playboy driver than any of his monochrome contemporaries. Relief that at two years short of 40, having scored one of the best wins of the 1997 season, he had survived this potentially hazardous activity.

The man, who was closer to Ayrton Senna than any other Grand Prix driver, knows just how lucky he is to have the rest of his life to look forward to. At the time of his last race, from the drivers who started with him in the Austrian Grand Prix in August 1984 – his Formula One debut – Berger was the only one still racing. In his career, he earned 11 pole positions, 20 fastest race laps, and clocked up over 4,000 Grand Prix kilometres, each one as treacherous as the next. 'I have a lot to be thankful for,' he said, 'most of all my health and sanity. I'm still alive and relatively unscathed. Thank God for that.'

Not that Berger is religious, in the usual sense of the word. On the contrary, he has, several times in the past, described himself as 'a non-believer' and 'sceptic', although never going as far as to call himself a full-blown atheist. It was only after his decision to quit Formula One that Berger actually started to think about, in his own words, 'a Supreme Being'.

'For a long time I never gave a second thought to life after death, God, or anything like that,' he said. 'But after I retired I started to think about spiritual things, maybe because I was perhaps subconsciously looking for something else to fill the void. Grand Prix racing gave me a huge thrill, I loved it; loved the buzz, the lifestyle, everything about it. But when Ayrton died, I started to look deep inside me for the true meaning of life. I examined my motives for pursuing such a dangerous career; I examined my own soul. It didn't stop me from enjoying myself but when I stopped I thought about these kind of things again and now, well maybe I do believe in another power.'

It is a little-known fact that Berger and Senna talked about the Christian faith. The Brazilian counted Berger among his closest, most trusted friends and together they shared their hopes and fears as well as a few moments of madness, mainly when Berger's wild sense of humour got the better of him.

The Austrian had a talent for collecting amphibian wildlife and hiding it in Ayrton Senna's hotel room, or filling his shoes with butter, sometimes glue. Berger was a habitual practical joker but Senna often responded in kind. The Brazilian had a carbon fibre briefcase; Berger tested its indestructibility by dropping it from the helicopter they were travelling in. Senna reacted by pinching Berger's credit cards and getting them drilled and bolted together with a huge nut and bolt. There were times when the pair laughed so hard they fell about in fits of hysterical ecstasy.

But when Senna died the laughing stopped. Berger was over-whelmed by a deep, painful sadness. It was almost too much for him to bear, especially when he remembered how anxious Senna had been before the last race of his life. The Brazilian had not only confided in his girlfriend but also in Berger. In truth Senna went to Berger to ease his troubled mind. The Austrian always seemed to make him feel a whole lot better, and Berger, more than most, somehow identified with and understood Senna's sixth sense, probably because he had experienced such things as premonition.

More than that even, Berger's whole demeanour put Senna at ease. Berger's competitive focus is softened by the human touch. He has a sense of irreverence which many find appealing. Senna certainly did. After his Benetton blitzed the opposition at the German Grand Prix one year the Williams technical director Patrick Head asked: 'Gerhard, why can't you drive like that in every race?'

Deadpan, Berger replied: 'Come off it, Patrick. You can't expect me to drive like that all the time.' And then he burst out laughing. Most drivers would have made excuses about the varying performance of their car. But not Berger, he had no such delusions of infallibility.

Gerhard Berger was born on 27 August 1959 in the town of Wörgl in the Tyrolean Alps. To imagine the environment 30 years ago, when Berger was growing up in the valleys of the Tyrol, it is helpful to know that the most popular hobby among the young men in his village was racing anything with a souped-up engine. By the age of seven, Berger had already begun to develop a keen interest in motorbikes and he fitted right into the scene.

In his father's courtyard, which doubled as a storage facility for his transport company, there were cars, trucks and machines, which provided Berger with everything he needed. His father was extremely understanding but when, at the age of 11, Gerhard asked if he could have his own moped, his father declined. 'How would it look to the police?' he told his disappointed son. When the boy broke his leg in a skiing accident, however, his father took pity on him. And 'to save the poor guy from limping around on his cast more than necessary', his father bought him a low-powered moped. That first moped could get up to about 80 kph. Later on, after putting pistons from boat motors into the engines, his mopeds could reach speeds of 110 and eventually 140 kph.

Then came the motorcycles. At the age of 18, he was zipping around at speeds of up to 270 kph. He remembers how 'we thought it was really cool' when, after driving long enough on the autobahn at 270 kph, the tyres would expand and rub against the fenders.

After training as a mechanic and working in his father's business as a long-distance truck driver, Berger abandoned the career he'd been striving for as a motorcycle racer and became addicted to the thrill and atmosphere of auto racing. He can't explain it in elaborate terms. It was simply that 'suddenly auto races were the thing'.

It began in 1980 with a Ford Escort. Then, with Alfasud, there were the Formula Three years from 1982 to 1984 where he learned all the basics needed to give a young man his start. John Nielsen, Emmanuele Pirro, Roberto Ravaglia, Martin Brundle, Pierluigi Martini and Ivan Capelli were his most important competitors at that time, but Ayrton Senna also crossed Berger's path during the Formula Three years.

Many years before Berger and Senna worked together, the Austrian, with only Formula Three and touring car experience, entered Formula One at the wheel of an ATS-BMW in 1984. The following year he raced for Arrows before switching to Benetton in 1986, when he scored his first win, in the Mexican Grand Prix.

His carefree manner and determined driving style struck a chord with Ferrari and he joined them in 1987. He stayed three years, winning four Grands Prix, during which he escaped with superficial burns after crashing his Ferrari at Imola in the 1989 San Marino race.

This same circuit was going to inflict on him terrible emotional wounds in 1994. In 24 hours, he would lose two close friends: fellow Austrian Roland Ratzenberger, a Formula One novice, and Ayrton Senna. Berger's emotions were in turmoil again 15 days later in Monaco following the accident of another Austrian, Karl Wendlinger, although the outcome was less traumatic with Wendlinger eventually waking from a two-week coma. During this time of great sadness and anxiety, Berger asked himself: 'Is it worth it?' He decided it was, so he carried on.

In 1990 he joined the McLaren team, where he partnered the dynamic Senna. Berger was hired as a replacement for Alain Prost, who had left because he could not handle Senna's dominance. Yet Berger proved to be different. Somehow he struck a chord with the ascetic Senna and the two men became deep personal friends. It was a real case of opposites attracting, the happy-go-lucky Berger helping Senna develop a sense of humour while Senna's obsessive attention to detail and total commitment taught Berger about developing his abilities as a driver.

Berger greatly admired the Brazilian. 'You know, in his mind, the only thing which existed was himself,' said Berger. 'He had to be first and, by this thinking, I believe he created a power.' In 1993 Berger left McLaren and returned to Ferrari. Yet the two men remained close friends.

Before climbing into his Williams FW16 for the San Marino Grand Prix Senna's last words to Frank Williams were: 'I've got to go and have a word with Gerhard.' Four hours later Berger would be the last person to visit Senna before he died.

Senna's death had a profound effect on Berger, more so perhaps because Senna's Christian faith had begun to rub off on him, but after a week he shrugged aside thoughts of retirement. He won the 1994 German Grand Prix for Ferrari but would not win again until 1997, his last season. By then he had switched back to Benetton and was already planning his retirement. After so many narrow escapes and, more significantly, so many tragedies, Berger realized that a man, no matter how lucky he may be, can only cheat death so many times. Sooner or later a risk worth taking becomes one risk too many, with little or no warning.

Suddenly the last of the playboys had grown old and wise. Of course Berger still retains the boyish enthusiasm and ambition which has fired him throughout his long and incident-filled Formula One career, but then, as it is with him now, Berger followed his head and not his heart. Even the quasi-supernatural premonitions that preceded races in Argentina and Germany were not reliable enough to persuade Berger that maybe he was blessed with good fortune. Common sense told him to get out while he was still in one piece and that is exactly what he did.

The theory that men who drive race cars develop some kind of highly tuned sixth sense is not lost on Berger, although he has often fallen into the trap of so many other drivers who ignore subliminal warnings – if such things exist. 'Maybe God was telling Ayrton not to race at Imola,' Berger said, 'and maybe this kind of premonition happens to us all. I can't explain it, but I have had one or two similar experiences, although not always warnings.'

Before the 1996 Argentina Grand Prix in Buenos Aires Berger had an uneasy feeling. He could not put his finger on exactly what it was; maybe he was coming down with something, or perhaps he was a little more tired or emotionally stressed than usual. But whatever it was it was real. A genuine sense of foreboding, so he ignored it.

What else could he have done, quit? No chance! During the first practice session of the meeting, Berger came round turn five at about 150 mph to discover a dog crossing the track ahead of his Benetton. Had they collided, Berger could have been killed, and the incident raised the spectre of the death of the great French driver Jean-Pierre Wimille in 1949. Wimille was killed when he swerved to miss a dog during practice for a Grand Prix in Buenos Aires. A track marshal reported that on his return to the garage Berger looked as though he had seen a ghost. 'He was as white as a sheet.'

The following season before the German Grand Prix at Hockenheim, Berger had another premonition. It was the same strong gut feeling, impossible to shake off or ignore, but impossible to diagnose. Berger knew he was going to win, even though he had not won a race for three years. Something inside him, or a force impacting on his psyche, or in his soul, said: 'Today you are going to win. Nothing can go wrong for you.' It was the same voice that had whispered a warning before the stray dog threatened to terminate Berger's existence at Buenos Aires.

'I can't explain why, but I knew I was going to win,' said Berger, 'it was a very strong feeling, very positive energy, and it happened after a very bad time in my life. I even had a dream about winning.'

The same thing happened to Ferrari driver Eddie Irvine before the first race of the 1999 Formula One season. Irvine experienced what can only be described as a surge of positive energy during the build-up to the Australian Grand Prix in Melbourne, which he won. He had an extraordinarily strong feeling that he would win and on the eve of the race two friends called him to say they had dreamt he would win. Uncanny.

For Berger, though, his win in the 1997 German Grand Prix was more than a dream come true. It was an answer to prayer. His final season, in the frequently troubled Benetton, was the most difficult of his career, salvaged only and marvellously by his success at Hockenheim at a time when he was being dismissed as a tired has-been.

It came at a moment when Berger seemed to be assailed on all sides by personal misfortune. It was his first outing after a three-race layoff grappling with acute sinus troubles and he had just been told by Benetton's managing director Flavio Briatore that his services would not be needed in 1998. On top of that his father was killed in an aircraft accident 10 days before the Hockenheim race and his mechanic and close friend suffered a heart attack.

He said: 'I was suddenly in the worst situation of my entire life. People were already retiring me, saying that I was not fit enough and not good enough any more. I was really looking forward to 1997 but I could not have asked for a worse start. Everything started to fall apart.

'At the back of my mind I suppose I realized that this could be my last and I wanted it to be a good one. I trained really hard through the winter and was confident and highly motivated. The first few races went quite well and then suddenly I got sinusitis. When I went to Imola for the San Marino Grand Prix I was heavy on antibiotics and from that moment my performances began to go.

'I was still second in the championship but I could not keep my physical condition and I realized that I had to go into hospital and miss three races. It was not just being in hospital. I could do no physical training and had to stay quiet. It was all very difficult but then came Hockenheim and suddenly it was as though a cloud had lifted. The way I felt, nothing could stand in my way. I just knew I was going to win.'

So three years after his last victory, and on the same high-speed circuit through the forests of Baden-Würtemberg, Gerhard Berger completed a remarkable comeback: claiming pole position, recording the fastest lap and securing the 10th victory of his long career, 17.5 seconds ahead of nearest rival Michael Schumacher's Ferrari.

'I seemed to find something extra, some extra powers,' said Berger, whose engine had expired at Hockenheim the previous year as he led with one lap to go. 'It was remarkable because I was not at peak fitness. I should not have had a chance really. At one stage, I really thought I would not finish when someone's engine [Barrichello's] blew in front of me and I almost stopped.'

It was an epic race for the veteran Austrian, arguably the best of his career, but one plagued by misfortune for many of the other drivers. Berger, demonstrating a perfect starting technique, made the most of the clear track ahead of the 12th pole position of his career to lead the way into the Nord Kurve. Behind him, Michael Schumacher tussled with Giancarlo Fisichella for second place, but was resisted and settled for third ahead of Hakkinen, Alesi and Villeneuve, who had catapulted his Williams-Renault into sixth place from ninth on the grid.

Tarso Marques' Minardi was the only car left standing at the start, but three men carrying high hopes of Hockenheim success quickly joined him on the sidelines. David Coulthard, in his Mercedes Benz-powered McLaren, skewered into a sandtrap, recovered, but then spun again amid the traffic, while Eddie Irvine, having made a formidable start, was removed when the front right wheel of Heinz-Harald Frentzen's Williams-Renault hit his Ferrari's left rear. Both were punctured and, after crawling back to the pits, like Coulthard, they retired – Irvine while his Italian mechanics dealt with a friction fire.

Berger reeled off five fastest laps in the opening nine and was 9.5 seconds clear of Fisichella at the end of lap 11 when Hill went into the pits, from 10th place, for the first time. Johnny Herbert's race was ended two laps earlier when his Sauber Petronas was apparently struck by Pedro Diniz's Arrows. Berger swept in for his first pit stop after 17 laps, Alesi having gone in one lap earlier from fifth, and he resumed fourth behind Fisichella (leading a Grand Prix for the first time), Schumacher and Hakkinen. Villeneuve was fifth and Trulli sixth, but as the stops sequence began, it was clear more changes lay ahead.

Fisichella retained command for seven laps before slithering towards the Jordan garage in such wild fashion that he careered briefly off-line, scattering the photographers like rabbits, before his 5.7 second stop. He resumed second, Berger rapidly advancing into a 17-second lead by the completion of lap 26, with Alesi third. The Benettons were showing Williams, with identical engines, the way at this stage. But with their drivers on multi-stop strategies, the outcome remained in the balance.

As the sun beat down, the processional progress may have become tedious, but not for Jan Magnussen. On lap 28 he retired when his Stewart-Ford suffered such a spectacular engine failure it appeared poised, by dint of the billowing smoke clouds, to perform an Apollo-style take-off. Two laps earlier, Hill had pitted for the second time, an act that left him a lap down on Berger in 11th. This was to be improved dramatically when, on lap 34, a variety of events coincided around the forested track.

First Villeneuve spun off at the first chicane, and then Rubens Barrichello copied his team-mate Magnussen's example and retired before Berger made his second pit stop. He took only 6.5 seconds but rejoined a few lengths behind Fisichella's yellow car. Not for long, however. Berger outbraked the Jordan at the third chicane to stamp his authority on proceedings once again with 10 laps to go.

Fisichella was in some trouble and this became apparent on lap 39 when he spun off at the entry to the stadium section. He had suffered a left rear puncture with which he struggled back to the pits. Schumacher took over second, then made a second splash-and-dash stop, resuming in pursuit of Berger. A fuel signal from the Benetton pits raised German hopes, but this time there was to be no repeat of the Austrian's misfortune of the previous year

'After I won I enjoyed the moment but a voice in my mind said, "No, no, you are going to retire at the end of the season," and that voice made it very clear to me. To be world champion was my dream but it did not happen and you cannot have everything. I can go away happy that I worked hard, had a good time, stayed alive and still in one piece with my sanity intact – well, more or less!

'In 14 years, a lot of things change, especially in this business. You change automatically. I am 40 now and older, of course, but I still try to take it pretty easy as always even though I am a bit more serious about some other things. I still like to go to the beach, I like winter sports and a bit of fun and danger. But not as much as I used to. I am more sensible now and have responsibilities.'

Berger is married to Anna-Maria and is the father of three young children. 'I tried very hard not to get married!' he added. 'I thought it would "clip my wings", but, in fact, I am very happy. I did not expect to see myself in this role as a father, but I have surprised myself. I thought marriage, for me, would be a disaster – but I am now very positive about it. The best thing, though, is being able to enjoy being a husband and father. I think of Ayrton and Roland and all the other guys who have been killed and realize how lucky I am. I thank God for my good fortune.'

## 13

# Nothing Stays the Same

*When he's ready to stop racing, I won't be sorry.*

GEORGIE HILL, 1998

Sometimes, in those quiet moments when time graciously appears to stand still to allow a man to take stock of his life, Damon Hill thought about his wife and children and wondered if he had any right at all to risk everything. He is not a religious man or even very superstitious but, in these intense flashes of consciousness when the danger and insanity of Formula One weighs heavy on the mind, Hill often found himself praying, silently, for safety. When a man lives such an extreme existence, this searching of the soul is inevitable.

Hill, world champion in 1996, is a borderline agnostic, someone who admits to often questioning the existence of God. But he knows, better than most, that not all things in life are as black and white as that chequered flag which he is prepared to risk life and limb to reach first. 'I believe in fate,' he says, 'but I'm not a fatalist, in the true sense of the word. I believe there is a God, but I'm not a religious man. I've got an open mind about what happens when a person dies. Maybe there is life after death, who knows, but one thing is certain, racing car drivers are not immune to feelings of mortality.

'Just because I accept the risks involved, including the possibility of death, doesn't mean we get used to the idea. I never dwell on it. I'm not a morbid kind of person. But sometimes I look around at what I've got, a beautiful wife and children, nice home, financial security, good health, and get kind of scared to think that I could lose it all in the blink of an eye. Each time there is a fatal accident in

Formula One, it shakes you up and makes you reassess the risks involved, and I am sure that it is the same for everyone connected with the sport. Nothing is worth the cost of a human life, not even this sport that I love so much.'

It is this appreciation of the value of the things in life we often take for granted, that drove Hill to one conclusion during the summer of 1999. The death of his friend and team-mate Ayrton Senna five years earlier was a warning about the inherent dangers of his chosen sport, and almost persuaded Hill to quit there and then. But it was a 100 mph crash into a concrete wall in the 1999 Canadian Grand Prix that finally helped Hill to decide to walk out of Formula One for the sake of his family. His wife, Georgie, watched for agonizing seconds until Hill jumped unharmed from his yellow Jordan, but in those moments she decided to encourage him to bring a surprise end to his career as one of Britain's best-known sportsmen.

The only man to emulate his father as Formula One world champion said his decision to leave his £4.5 million-a-year contract with the Benson & Hedges Jordan team is irreversible. Only time will tell if this is true, but if Hill's deep concern for the wellbeing of his family is anything to go by, he is unlikely to return to Formula One. Perhaps the most telling line in his brief announcement midway through the 1999 Grand Prix season was dedicated to his wife. It said simply: 'I would especially like to thank my wife, Georgie, who has had the greatest burden to bear. I love you.'

Hill, approaching 40, plans to make up for lost time. During the final three years of his racing career he was away from his home in Ireland for up to 250 days a year. The dangerous and gruelling Grand Prix schedule took Hill away from his children – Oliver, nine, Joshua, seven, Tabitha, three, and Rosie, one – too often. During the months before he escaped from his crash at the Canadian Grand Prix, Hill feared motor racing might take him away from them forever. As he walked away from the crumpled wreck of his car on the afternoon of Sunday 13 June 1999, Hill knew he had to get out.

Hill was increasingly distracted by the pull of home and family in a dangerous sport that demands absolute dedication. He has won the world championship and 22 Grands Prix. He wants to enjoy the memory and be glad that he can. 'Enough is enough,' he said. 'My wife and children need me and I need them. I don't want them to worry any more. It's not worth it. There is too much at stake.'

Motor racing, according to Damon's father, the late Graham Hill, is 'like shooting the rapids while balancing an egg on a spoon'; virtually impossible. But this is precisely the point, to be a successful racing driver you must learn to live in this 'nearly' world where the line between what is possible and what is not is measured in terms of sheer will power and little else. Of course, technology plays a part in pushing back the boundaries of achievement, but strength of mind, the ability to squeeze out another drop of courage and stamina at the point of human tolerance, is the key. Sheer will power is perhaps the real difference between life and death on the track, even though survival in this highly dangerous sport is sometimes dependent on luck, good and bad.

No matter how cool and calculating a driver is, no matter how brave and skilful, he will never be the master of luck. Good or bad fortune is a law unto itself. Human ability or mechanical excellence does not govern it; it does not adhere to the rules of physics or respect the theory of chance. Luck will kill or spare a life with no consideration for what should or shouldn't be or what is right or wrong. If a man is the best driver in the world with the best safety record, the highest skill rating and the greatest courage, luck will kill him as quickly and mercilessly as the driver who has the least chance of surviving or thriving. Luck doesn't care either way.

One afternoon in the summer of 1997, long before he called it quits, luck played a cruel trick on Damon Hill, as if to prove how easily it can make or break a human life. Perhaps cruel is the wrong word – luck is either good or bad or nothing at all. On this day in question, in the life of Damon Hill, it was largely good and for a moment innocuously bad. Had the instant of ill fortune been harmful then Hill might not have lived to see the funny side.

It was during and after practice at Silverstone, before the British Grand Prix, and Hill, the defending world champion, was putting his Arrows team car through its paces at the famous English track. Silverstone is probably one of the greatest circuits on the Grand Prix calendar, possessing an excellent variety of corners, some longish straights and wide, smooth tarmac which makes the whole lap very challenging. Quite simply, Silverstone is an incredibly exciting ride, particularly Copse Corner, which in Hill's own words 'is awesome'.

It has traditionally been a fast circuit and this is what people like about it. All the drivers like going round Silverstone. It's a bit like the notorious Spa in Belgium – very fast and very dangerous. There have been lots of improvements to the circuit during the past few years which have made it both faster and safer, but it's still got one hell of a bite.

Watching Hill's Arrows hurtling through Copse Corner made me realize just how high the stakes are in this dangerous game of guts and glory. Copse had been opened out a lot and was once again a very fast fifth gear bend, taken almost 'flat' at about 155 mph. One mistake and you're history. Hill rode his luck a couple of times going through Copse but on both occasions the car responded favourably, staying on the track instead of introducing Hill to the fence. Then, in the skip of a heartbeat, he'd streak up to the quick Maggotts/Becketts section, which is traditionally one of the best places in the world to watch a Formula One car and see just what it can do. The speed at which they go through these left-right-left-right curves is enormously fast (from 175 mph down to 100 mph in sixth, fifth and then fourth gears).

The cars demonstrate an incredible amount of grip, pulling between 3G and 4G, and really performing to the physical maximum in this section. There is an opportunity to overtake down Hangar Straight. If you get a good exit out of Becketts there is always an area where if you get a little bit of extra horsepower it is possible. Accelerating down the Hangar Straight he reached almost 190 mph before braking into Stowe Corner. It is a very quick corner, fourth gear and 100 mph with no margin for error. Down the slope to Vale, which has not changed and is the slowest bend (second gear and 55 mph). Next, on the way out of Club Corner you have to use a lot of delicate throttle and control the balance of the car, because it picks up speed all the way through the corner and there is always a place in mid-bend where there is too much power and not enough grip – and the car wants to oversteer.

Then you power up the hill at 180 mph and into the Abbey section where it is difficult to see the apex of the bend. Abbey Corner is a 90-degree left with a kink on the exit, which is a bit too slow. On one lap Hill accelerated hard over the brow and into Bridge Bend in fifth gear at about 150 mph, pulling over 4G, and almost lost it. He hadn't time to react and it was only luck that prevented him from crashing. On another day, he may not be so lucky, especially in a race with other cars on the track.

Out of Priory and into the long last bend of the lap at Luffield, Hill's car is sliding as he puts all the power down on exit. A good exit will determine maximum speed over the finish line, ideally reaching over 175 mph in sixth gear before braking for Copse and heading off on another lap. A couple of times through Luffield he rides his luck again, but gets away with it. Afterwards, Hill had the look of a man who knew he'd been fortunate to survive the session without coming unstuck, but ironically his luck was about to run out. On the way out of the car park, Hill made a mistake which resulted in a collision with a parked car at 5 mph. Luck had deserted him, at just the right moment!

Maybe this is the way it's going to be for Hill. Luck on the track, no luck off it, although it would be an awfully sad irony for any racing driver to get killed in a car wreck on the way to Sainsbury's. Hill, touch wood, has a knack of walking away from accidents on and off the track and he has had more than his fair share of smashes, most of which, ironically, took place before he became a professional racing driver.

Hill, now a millionaire tax exile living in Ireland, has owned a great variety of road cars: 'old heaps, second-hand cars and company cars', and he first drove a car at the age of eight, sitting on his father's lap in a Land Rover, just steering. 'But, by myself, it was in a Mini Cooper S,' he recalls, 'when I was about 11 ... down our drive. We had quite a long drive and it was for a film about my father. A life story thing in about 1971.

'They said, "Can we get you driving down there?" and I said, "Okay, I can do that." I don't think my father was there at the time – and I don't think I'd ever driven before in my life. So I came haring down the drive in this Mini and screeched to a halt and then jumped out with the engine still running and the car in gear.'

Motorbikes rather than cars were to become the passion of his teenage years. 'I passed my driving test in St Albans, at the first attempt, after two or three weeks of lessons with the BSM,' he recalled. 'Most of my lessons were done after school in the winter when it was dark and when I took the test it was in the daytime and everything seemed completely different. Luckily, I didn't get anything wrong.

'I think I took the test in an Allegro, or something horrible like that. My mum had a bright green Ford Cortina two-litre. A mark 4, maybe. It was a Ghia and an automatic – which was the first car I borrowed and used to hammer about the place. I was still at school, of course. I rode my bike into school every day and used the car for messing about.

'I had no feelings towards cars at all. They kept the rain off, but that was it. I did end up buying a Fiat 124 Special, which was lightning quick, and had a brilliant engine in it – a 1600 DOHC. Eventually a wheel fell off as I was turning left into Seymour Street in London. I dragged it to the side of the road and that was the last I ever saw of it. I just abandoned it.'

Hill, like most 19-year-olds, thought he was going to live forever. 'That was quite a dangerous period of my life,' he recalled. 'The Fiat would do 120 mph. I couldn't understand why the guy in front wasn't going any faster and would object when I overtook him and cut in three inches in front of him.'

'I was constantly stopped for speeding and minor misdemeanours. I was always on the border with the points, but never quite enough for a ban. Until 1995 I had never had a ban.' The year before he became Formula One world champion Hill was fined and banned for one week for doing 101 mph on his way to an appearance on BBC *Pebble Mill at One* ... it was twenty to, he said, and he had a long way to go.

'I was in disgrace,' he said. 'But Georgie said she wasn't surprised. It happens to everyone eventually. To do 70 mph on a motorway these days is to be the next thing to a saint.'

It wouldn't have been possible in the car he got after the Fiat – a 1964 VW Beetle bought for £200 when he was living in Wandsworth, south London. 'It was very easy to push and start, which was a good thing, because I had to do that a lot. I had great fun in it, but mostly when it was snowing because it had rear wheel drive and you could get the most fantastic power slides everywhere.

'It had all the weight at the back, which stepped out on you every time you went round a corner. You were only doing 55 mph, but you felt as if you were doing 155 mph. But when it rained all the electrics failed and the windscreen wiper stopped.'

Next he bought a Ford Transit. Salt water from fish, the previous owner's stock-in-trade, had rusted the rear, and given the interior something of an aroma. Hill recalls that £500 changed hands. He later discovered that the sliding door slid all the way off its runners.

'It meant I would arrive home at night, having driven from Cadwell Park or somewhere, swing back the door ... and it would crash to the floor and wake up all the neighbours. I'd then spend half an hour trying to get the door back on.' Hill found it easier to change gear without using the clutch – which may have helped his driving technique – and was particularly attached to the van's paint scheme.

'It had yellow sides with white at the bottom and red on part of the roof. But not all the way across the roof. I only found this out when I looked down from my bedroom window: it was only red as far as the guy could reach while, obviously, standing on the floor. It had a patch of white in the middle and the red went only as far as his arms could stretch ...'

The fish van is one of Hill's more comical motoring memories but, on a more solemn note, his first serious spin occurred in a Ford Granada 2.3 estate car. He was going to see a friend in Bushey, and was going round the roundabout by the M1. 'I had this large speaker cabinet in the back and I was ... well, enjoying the horsepower,' Hill said. 'The speaker cabinet slid to the back of the car and gave it a pendulum effect. I ended going up the motorway slip road backwards and cars were coming off the motorway towards me. I was very lucky.'

There have been others, and not just on the track. Inspired by watching rallying on television, the young Hill took his mother's Ford Fiesta 1300 Special. 'It was pouring with rain and I thought I was Hannu Mikkola,' he recalled. 'I came hammering down this hill and lost it. Some idiot was stopped on the hill to turn right, and I didn't manage to miss him.'

By this time Hill was well on his way to becoming the ultimate boy racer, fuelled by the sort of reckless passions he would eventually pursue round Grand Prix circuits. Hill was not destined to head down the road to the land of normality where dreams are fenced round with mortgages, pushchairs, job worries and babysitters, a prison of responsibility where passion is regulated and never reckless.

Quite where a soft spot for speed turned into a serious tilt at single-seater racing is not hard to pinpoint. Hill would like you to believe that it wasn't necessarily fate and that one thing led to another – and, hey presto, glory's finger beckons. His father Graham Hill has to take a share of the credit for sowing the seeds of Damon's need for speed, but his wife Georgie deserves more for not putting her foot down long before her husband's.

Hill became world champion at the age of 36, which is two years younger than the last British driver to win the title, Nigel Mansell in 1992. Despite the air of inevitability it brought, there was no doubt that Hill had come a long way fast. Once he arrived in Formula One, that is. His achievement came only four years after his Formula One race debut behind the wheel of a tank-like Brabham at the 1992 French Grand Prix.

It was as much a triumph for Georgie Hill as for Damon, who could not have done it without the support of a very understanding and also courageous partner. Behind every successful man ... goes the saying and like father, like son – Graham Hill was also fortunate to have a wife who not only encouraged his reckless passion but supported it with strength of mind and a spirit to match. In the face of such danger there is no place for division; either both partners accept the risks involved or none at all.

Four years after his Formula One debut Damon Hill did what most of us can only dream about – not as the son of the only driver to win the world championship, the Indianapolis 500 and the Le Mans 24-hour race, the dashing debonair who played golf with President Nixon, quipped to order and danced on tables with no trousers on – but as his own man. A driver seen by his supporters as an ordinary guy made good and the husband of a woman who represents the reality of the fast-paced madness of motor racing. Every time Damon Hill went racing, Georgie accepted it could be the last time she or their four children would ever see him alive again. Maybe this is why they have such a strong love and a deep understanding of life outside racing; this and their gritty, unassuming realism.

They are one of the more balanced couples in the sport and Georgie has been with Damon through it all – from the heart-pounding excitement of his debut and subsequent championship success to the heart-chilling fear and tragedy of Imola 1994 – and has seen the life behind the headlines. She has congratulated and consoled, laughed and cried, and helped plot a course through the intrigues and deceptions which pass for normality in Formula One.

They live in a fine house in Killiney Bay, just south of Dublin. When they are with each other they make the most of it, as do the majority of motor racing's couples. The 1998 Formula One champion Mika Hakkinen told me: 'The time I spend with my wife Erja is very, very important to me. We make the most of every second we are together.' Gerhard Berger felt the same way before he quit and so did Ronnie Peterson, before he was killed. Many other leading Formula One drivers echoed the sentiment. It is as though they are grateful for each second of life outside the seeming insanity of the sport they pursue with such dangerous ambition.

Damon and Georgie Hill have been together for nearly 20 years and there have been many big changes in their lives, especially in the past 10 years. Damon Hill has gone from being a lowly paid van driver to a global celebrity with his own private jet. Formula One is a world of swerving fortunes and shifting loyalties. Nothing stays the same. For this reason, home life is an important concept for Hill. His wife and children represent the place that doesn't change, vital security. Before he decided to quit, the quiet days had been vital to Hill's equilibrium. Because however tough they look, most racing drivers are insecure. Formula One is as ruthless as it is dangerous, a very extreme experience for those in the spotlight; the highs are very high and the lows very, very low.

In 1998 Georgie Hill said: 'Our everyday home life has not really ever changed. The only thing is, the more successful Damon has become, the less time we've had to waste. We make the most of everything because we only have a short time to enjoy ourselves. Time pressure is the biggest thing hanging over us and the fear of something going wrong. He wants to be with us as much as we want to be with him. We love being together as a family and we are very proud and supportive of him.

'I told him that I could only cope with him racing as long as he was enjoying it. If anything were to happen to him, God forbid, and I knew at the time that he was not enjoying what he was doing, then it would break my heart. I accept the risks, we both do, but we don't dwell on them. When he's ready to stop racing, I won't be sorry but while he's still racing he has my full support. He deserves it.'

Hill may have been born to silver trophy cars, pushed around the garden in a toddler's pedal car by Jim Clark and Stirling Moss and spent his formative years in a 32-room country house full of his famous father's memorabilia. But his championship story, with its family misfortunes and public wobbles and spins, has been proverbial rags-to-riches stuff.

It will not just be that the former dispatch rider from London made himself one of the all-time top ten Grand Prix winners. The point is: throughout his early racing career, nothing was expected of him at all. And he has turned that around brilliantly.

Looking back over his childhood in *Damon Hill's Grand Prix Year* (Pan, 1995), his diary of the 1994 season, it is clear his father's profession held no allure. He recalls being summoned from a game in the garden to watch him win the 1969 Monaco Grand Prix on television. 'I only watched the last bit as he crossed the line; I was more interested in getting back to playing my game. It was almost a case of "He's won a race; so what?"'

Motor sport was something that monopolized visitors' conversation and kept father from son. 'My bedroom was above his office, so I could hear him on the phone,' he recalled. 'I knew when he was there and I used to go into the office and spend a long time listening to him – you could never get the chance to actually talk to him.'

His youth was wallpapered with racing paraphernalia, and it was the antithesis of excitement. 'The races were very long and usually very boring.' Everything had a motor racing context. On one occasion, having badgered his father for a Honda monkey bike, he found himself invited to Brands Hatch where Graham Hill unveiled one in a surprise presentation. 'I was very embarrassed that he had done it in front of an audience; everyone was there to see me get this thing. I felt awkward because there was always a fuss about everything associated with him – and now I was part of it.'

A trial on an off-road bike fired an addiction to the beauty of two-wheeled racing. Cars were ugly, he thought somewhat rebelliously. Posters of Evel Knievel went up and, even after his father was killed in an aeroplane crash at Elstree in 1975, plunging the family into financial ruin, the compulsion to race, to take obvious risks, was so strong that he sawed the side-stand off his road bike, camped out in a tent and entered his first club race at Lydden Hill in Kent. The experience only made him determined to find a race bike. In a realization that was to recur when he started racing cars, 21-year-old Hill saw belatedly that he had not thought through his approach.

'I used to think you simply jumped on the bike, went like stink – and became Barry Sheene. I really had my head in the clouds ... I was doing it completely blind and refusing any help. No one I knew went bike racing and I was either too stupid or too proud to ask anyone else. I just blundered on ... until I suddenly realized that there were other elements to this business; it was all about state of mind and being prepared.'

His mother, naturally worried about the dangers of bike racing, paid for him to attend a course at the Winfield Elf racing school in Magny Cours, where he showed natural aptitude. 'At first I thought the cars were pretty horrible-looking things but, once in the cockpit, I forgot all that because they were quite good fun to drive.'

And there began the pragmatic eight-year trawl through Formula Ford, British Formula Three, Formula 3000 and test driving where any private dreams of emulating his father's verve were quashed by the need to make money. In 1988 Hill had bought a house, and his wife Georgie had to give up work following the birth of their first son, Oliver, who had Down's syndrome.

The turning point of his career was a decade ago. Having led more than 50 per cent of his races for the Middlebridge Formula 3000 team and started most of them from the front row (but not won a race), Frank Williams gave him the job as Williams test driver.

Much has been made of Hill's failure to win championships at junior level or even to accrue many race wins. He has admitted that he has had to learn that most basic of racing skills – overtaking in the thick of a contest – as he was clocking up Grand Prix starts simply because he had never karted.

The financially bleak learning curve of Hill's early years was not without its highlights. After a fifth place in the Formula Ford Festival in 1984 he won the Best Newcomer award. The mistake of bypassing Formula 2000 and then spending three long seasons in Formula Three, instead of the traditional stepping-stone year, was amended when Hill ended up with Ulsterman Martin Donnelly as team-mate in 1987.

'That perked me up,' he explained. 'He was highly rated and I knew it would be good for me to have him in the team – rather like 1993 and 1994 in Formula One; you raise your game to match your team-mate. Donnelly kept the pressure on me and I learnt a great deal racing against him.'

Raising the game is something he has done tenaciously ever since. The break in British Formula 3000, which required the large budget Hill could never muster, came when he least expected it, and he supplemented competition with paid touring car drives and a share of a Porsche at Le Mans. Again, a one-off experience added to his armoury.

'It was one of the most exciting things I had ever done; driving at night, going round and round, watching the dials, just trying to do the job ... all they wanted was for me to do the job right; no heroics or anything like that. It was far removed from driving a Formula One car and yet this was just the sort of attitude needed when I started testing for Williams a few years later.'

'His determination is amazing,' said Georgie. 'There have been lots of times when it did not look all that promising. I remember the day when he came back from the Magny Cours racing school and told me he was going to become Formula One world champion. I thought it was something else he simply wanted to do. But he stuck to it, refused to be diverted. There were times over the last six years when matters were desperate, but Damon always stayed positive and kept thinking forward.'

The toughest time of his career, with the exception of Imola 1994, was at the end of his two-year dogfight with Michael Schumacher, when Frank Williams and Patrick Head, never the sport's most compassionate managers of men, decided that he wasn't quite pulling his weight. Georgie Hill recalled: 'There was one brief moment when he thought: "I'm not enjoying this any more and I want to stop." It was 1995, the year Williams lost the championship. I think he felt very abandoned by Frank and Patrick. The papers were out for the kill, which we could not understand at the time, considering he was a British driver. There was no support at all and I think he found it very hard to deal with.

'He thought he was out there doing a job as a racing driver, and suddenly he was being criticized for a hundred and one other things he did not realize came with the job. It was very hard for us. We were moving to Ireland, I was heavily pregnant and he was caught up in trying to win the championship with no support from the team's hierarchy. He was not enjoying it and was talking about quitting.'

He didn't. He won the final race that year in Adelaide and over the winter got fitter, stronger and tougher. He'd been hurt by a lot of different things so that afterwards nothing could really hurt him again. He started strongly the following year and ended up Formula One world champion in 1996.

The dream had come true and everyone was happy, especially Georgie. More than anything she wanted her husband to follow in his father's footsteps, irrespective of the risks involved. Damon also rarely gave a second thought to the potential consequences of competing in the world's most dangerous sport. He'd seen it all, accidents, near misses and tragedy, but it was never enough to persuade him to walk away. He counted himself among life's chosen few, those lucky enough to make their dreams real and not fantasy.

But not before the 1994 San Marino Grand Prix, the blackest weekend in Formula One, when the awful emptiness and loss of death without hope led Damon Hill to the very edge of his own sanity. For the first time in his motor racing career – if only for a short while – Damon Hill wanted to quit. He examined his own motives for pursuing such a deadly obsession and they fell away, like so many dead leaves in a cold wind, fragile and useless. He was destined to become a champion like his father. But at what price?

# 14

# World of Pain

*It's not as if racing drivers don't know that fatal accidents are a possibility. If a driver does not accept that fact, if he is completely and utterly shocked by a fatal accident, so much so that he cannot get back in a racing car, then he has been deluding himself about the danger up until that point.*

DAMON HILL, 1997

Damon Hill was Ayrton Senna's Williams-Renault team-mate when the Brazilian died in May 1994. The memory of what happened on that bloody Sunday at Imola will stay with Hill for the rest of his life, and the spectre of death that chilled each and every one of the drivers involved occasionally returns to haunt Hill. Time heals wounds, mental and physical, but rarely erases emotional scars.

The first shock for Hill during the blackest weekend came when Rubens Barrichello crashed during the opening qualifying session at Imola. He lost control of his Jordan coming through the last chicane, probably at around 160 mph, and didn't have time to correct the car. He shot over a kerb, which launched him into the air and then sent the Jordan barrel-rolling along the tyre barrier.

'What shook us most,' Hill recalls in *Damon Hill's Grand Prix Year*, 'was the rate at which the car took off; at one stage it looked as if it was going to smash through the fence and fly into the grandstand. The Jordan, more by luck than anything else, finished on its side, upside down and against the barrier. That was bad enough but the marshals promptly tipped the car over and, as it crashed on to its bottom, you could see Barrichello's head thrashing around in the cockpit.'

It was a stomach-churning sight and also provoked anger and

disbelief among many of the drivers competing in the race. 'I was astonished that the marshals should have done that,' Hill added, 'particularly in view of the neck and spinal injuries received by J.J. Lehto and Jean Alesi during test sessions earlier in the year. After an accident like that, Barrichello could have sustained similar injuries. He should have been left as he was or, if there was a risk of fire, then at least the car should have been put down gently.'

The next day, Barrichello was walking around the paddock with nothing more than a cut lip and a broken nose. He was talking about making a comeback at the next race. The incident, despite its worrying implications, was gradually forgotten as Grand Prix racing got back down to business. In the case of Hill and Senna that meant continuing their efforts to improve the Williams FW16.

Despite having tested at Nogaro in the southwest of France during the days leading up to Imola, the pair were still concerned about the FW16. There had been a certain amount of educated guesswork and, while everyone tried to be optimistic, Hill and Senna were sceptical. 'We couldn't honestly say that the car was going to be any better than it had been,' Hill said.

The problem was fundamentally twofold. First, the car was not consistently quicker than the Benetton and second, it felt horrible to drive. It is arguable which of the two problems made Hill and Senna more unhappy, but it was most probably the former. 'We were always changing the set-up of the car in an attempt to find that perfect combination which would turn the promise of a great car into a reality,' said Hill. 'What we wanted from the FW16 was a feeling of balance and driveability.'

These are the conditions which enable a driver to enjoy the experience of driving and consequently go faster. It is difficult to become familiar with a car if it is constantly being changed in an attempt to get good performance – it becomes a vicious circle, although Hill revealed: 'Ayrton had enormous reserves of ability and could overcome deficiencies in a chassis. Also, it is more common to have a car which is difficult than one which is perfect.

'So, in some ways, things were as they should have been at Imola. It was a pleasant surprise to find on the first day of practice that things had improved slightly. I was looking forward to really making some progress with the car even though I had one or two nerve-racking moments when I had to take to the grass because of a difficulty with the brakes.'

At the end of the first practice day it was discovered that there had been a problem with Hill's car. He had gone off at the final corner and damaged the suspension. By the time repairs had been carried out, there were just 10 minutes of the first qualifying session remaining and Hill only managed seventh place on the provisional grid. Even so, he still felt good about the Williams although Senna did not share his optimism. 'He was not convinced we were going in the right direction,' Hill said. 'In other words, he didn't like certain aspects of the car's behaviour. But then he was a perfectionist.'

On Saturday, the day before the 1994 San Marino Grand Prix, the FW16 performed much better. On Hill's first quick laps during qualifying, he managed to pull himself up to fourth place. It had been a decent run and he was on his way in when he came across warning flags at the end of the 200 mph straight.

He got to Tosa corner, only to be confronted by the remains of Roland Ratzenberger's Simtek. Hill could see where the debris had started and, judging by the distance travelled, it was obvious that this had been a very big accident. As Hill went by, he had a strong sense of foreboding about Ratzenberger's condition because there was so much destruction. 'With Barrichello we had been lucky,' said Hill. 'But this time it was very clear that poor Roland was not going to be let off so lightly.'

It was an ominous sign and, unbeknown to everyone, the start of a terrible sequence of events which would demonstrate in no uncertain terms the inherent dangers of the sport. Practice was stopped. Senna, deeply disturbed by Ratzenberger's fate, went down to the site of the accident because he wanted to see for himself what had happened. He had done it before when Martin Donnelly crashed at Jerez in 1990 and it is every driver's right to do so if they wish; an unwritten code of conduct.

But not all drivers feel that way. Hill is one of them and chose not to visit the scene of the accident. He had been present at Goodwood during a Formula Three test session in February 1986 when Bertrand Fabi was killed and he had no wish to see anything like that again. Fabi's awful death had a profound effect on Hill. It had made him think about quitting. But that was a long time ago and the memory was well and truly buried. He did not want to stir such a painful emotion.

'Everyone was terribly concerned for Roland; the feeling was that he was in a bad way,' Hill remembered. 'When Ayrton returned, he spoke to Williams manager Patrick Head and me in private at the side of the motorhome. He said quite simply that Roland was dead. It was his way of getting the point across to us as deliberately as possible that from what he had witnessed there was no doubt about it. Then he went into the motorhome and changed out of his driving overalls even though the session was about to restart.'

Hill was in emotional turmoil and could not decide what the right thing to do should be; stop like Ayrton or soldier on? He wished the officials had cancelled the rest of the session so as to remove that particular dilemma. It had been left to him to decide whether or not he wished to go out again. 'You are immediately confronted with the question, "Do I get back into a racing car now – tomorrow – a week later – or never again?" Just how do you decide?' Hill said.

'It's not as if racing drivers don't know that fatal accidents are a possibility. If a driver does not accept that fact, if he is completely and utterly shocked by an accident like Ratzenberger's, so much so that he cannot get back in a racing car, then he has been deluding himself about the danger up until that point.

'Of course, racing drivers are not that stupid. But, when confronted with something like this, you are facing a severe and immediate test of whether or not you are prepared to accept the risk. Roland had said he was never as happy as when he got his Formula One drive. It's what he wanted to do. It's what a lot of people want to do and many never get the opportunity. Even so, that does not make situations such as this any easier to accept.'

The impact on Formula One of what happened during this May weekend in 1994 can be measured in shock and sadness alone. The fear and pain went deep into the psyche of the sport and everyone was deeply affected. In the immediate aftermath of Ratzenberger's death Williams and Benetton withdrew for the rest of the afternoon; others decided to continue with the session. But the question everyone was asking was, 'Why did Roland die?'

Hill admitted: 'There was concern that we had got to the point where the inherent risks in Formula One had become greater because of certain factors such as the speed of the cars and their increasing ability to withstand impacts. Something has to give and, in the light of recent accidents, it was turning out to be the driver.

'Had we reached the totally unacceptable stage where, if a car was going to hit a wall, then the driver was going to die?'

Ironically, in the light of what would happen the following day, Senna went to talk with other drivers and people such as Niki Lauda, who had been involved in a horrific accident in 1976. They wanted to know what could be done – and done immediately – about safety. It was agreed that the drivers should meet and discuss these matters, probably at Monaco in two weeks' time.

The mood that night was sombre to say the least. Hill stayed at the circuit, ate at the motorhome and generally found it difficult to think of much else but the accident. He tried to concentrate hard on what the Williams team were going to do for the race. His thoughts were, 'Look, I'm not going to stop racing; I'm looking forward to the Grand Prix. I enjoy my motor racing just as Roland did. Every second you are alive, you've got to be thankful and derive as much pleasure from it as you can.'

'In some ways,' Hill said, 'events that afternoon had been a spur, a reminder not to become complacent. It prompted me to be as positive as I could, look forward to the race and pray that something could be done to prevent such things happening again. It was to be a short-lived hope.'

When the cars went out for the warm-up on race morning, Sunday 1 May 1994, it was the first time Hill had been on the circuit since knowing the outcome of Roland's accident. It was a terrifying experience to go past the point where he had crashed. 'You could suddenly imagine the force of the impact,' Hill revealed, 'because you were actually travelling at the same speed he had been doing before he went off.'

Under normal circumstances, a Grand Prix driver wouldn't give it a second thought because, even though speeds reach 200 mph, it is not a part of the circuit where they come close to the limit; it is not a place they would worry about. 'You are relying entirely on the car,' Hill added, 'and, in the light of Ratzenberger's accident [probably caused by a failure of the nose wing mounting], it brings it home that sometimes you are just a passenger, putting your faith in the components.

'Drivers can accept the penalty of making a mistake; there is always the hope that they can do something about retrieving the situation and that the penalty is not too severe. At least it's their mistake. However, it feels very uncomfortable placing all your trust in the machinery – but there is no alternative. It is rather like being on an aeroplane; you are at the mercy of the pilot and the integrity of the equipment. You are powerless to do anything about your situation.

'At least I had the consolation of driving for Williams Grand Prix Engineering. I knew they would always do the best job possible. I knew, too, that Ayrton was out to dominate proceedings on race day. He had been fastest during the warm-up and I was next, nine-tenths of a second slower. I was happy with the car and I knew exactly what I'd had to do to set that time. So it was clear that Ayrton must have tried very hard indeed to set his time.'

It seemed to Hill that his team-mate was playing a psychological game here because, when you know that someone is almost a second a lap faster, it can demoralize you before the race has even started. Hill was not too worried because he was happy with the pace he was running at; he knew he could keep that up throughout the race whereas he didn't think Senna could. It was going to be a very interesting race.

All of this kept Hill's mind focused on the job but, when he and Senna went to the pre-race drivers' briefing, the previous day's tragedy proved to be just beneath the surface of everyone's consciousness. There was a minute's silence for Ratzenberger and the atmosphere was heavy with more than the usual pre-race tension. The talk of a drivers' meeting about safety to take place before Monaco rang alarm bells with the Formula One organizers. Whenever drivers group together there is the potential for trouble.

There was very little that could actually be achieved right then. Gerhard Berger raised one seemingly insignificant but relevant point about safety, but what he did not reveal was that he had been put up to it by Senna. The Brazilian didn't want to be the first to raise the point for fear of appearing to be the only person concerned about the problem, yet, typically, it was he who pressed it home. One of the things which had upset Senna six months earlier during the Japanese Grand Prix at Suzuka had been the introduction of a pace car during the final parade lap leading to the start.

He felt that it was no more than a gimmick and contributed nothing other than making the cars run far too slowly, thus rendering it less easy to get their tyres heated up. When other drivers backed him up, the officials agreed without hesitation to abandon that idea. A small victory had been won, but it was nonetheless significant. It was evidence of a failure to consult the drivers on important issues. There are certain matters which only the drivers are qualified to comment on; this strengthened the view that they should get together and express their fears in an attempt to have things changed and make the racing a little bit safer.

As the race at Imola approached, however, most drivers were able to put those thoughts to the back of their minds. Everyone felt – as they had done for the previous 12 years – that the dangers had been reduced considerably, to the point where death was but a slim possibility. And, in the aftermath, it was felt that Ratzenberger's crash had been one accident in a decade and it was unlikely to happen again for a while. 'You could claim that it is stupid to act like that,' Hill said. 'But that's the way people think. In any case, I'm sure Ayrton had other things to occupy him at this stage.'

It is true that Senna was feeling more than a little tense. Pressure had been coming from all directions. The media had been making a point about how the winner at Imola nearly always goes on to take the championship; that Senna had failed to score a single point in the first two races (something he had never experienced before in his 10 years in Formula One); that Michael Schumacher was the coming man and had a 20-point lead over Senna; that this was a crucial race because Schumacher and Benetton were favourites to win the next round at Monaco. All of that had impressed itself upon Senna. The warm-up had shown he was in a fighting mood. He had pole position and he was raring to turn the tide.

'Some people have attempted to infer that Ayrton was not in the right frame of mind for the race,' said Hill, 'but I cannot say anything more than that, to me he seemed totally focused. It must have been difficult completely to ignore the events of the day before, even for a man such as Ayrton, but when a race is about to start your mind can be on one thing only – winning.'

Sure enough, Senna made a good start but the race only got as far as the Acque Minerali chicane at the top of the circuit when the red flags came out and there were signs that the safety car was being brought into play. The safety car had been a fairly recent innovation, a means of slowing the cars as they formed a line behind an official car and circulated at reduced pace until the problem on the track had been sorted out. In this case, when the race got to the start/finish area, the drivers could see there had been a collision.

J. J. Lehto, starting from the second row, had stalled and had been hit from behind by Pedro Lamy, who had performed some sort of extraordinary manoeuvre from the penultimate row and crashed into the back of the Benetton. Hill had been warned on the radio that there was a lot of wreckage on the track but he was not aware that a wheel and parts of a car had cleared the fence and gone into the enclosure, injuring a number of spectators. There was debris everywhere and it was difficult to avoid it.

The aim of the safety car is to keep the show going without bringing the race to a complete halt. But the general feeling among Formula One drivers is that this should only have applied during a race once it was up and running. In this case, they hadn't even done a full lap at racing speed and it was difficult to see why the race could not have been stopped and restarted, as permitted by the rules. The result was that they were forced to go round at what can only be described as a snail's pace for five laps. The experience was frustrating to the point of exasperation for Senna. It was the last thing he needed, and as he cursed the futility of it all the nagging disquiet in his soul began to eat away at his usual ice-cool confidence.

# 15

# It Makes No Difference

*Motor racing is everything to me. Life would be empty without it.*

ROLAND RATZENBERGER, SIX MONTHS BEFORE HIS DEATH

Anyone who worked with Ayrton Senna will tell you how much time and effort he put into making sure his tyre pressures were absolutely right. It is no exaggeration to say that he could tell, to within half a pound p.s.i., whether the car was balanced or not. This is a critical area because every racing car is sensitive to tyre pressures.

While drivers wait on the grid during the final fifteen minutes or so, the tyres are wrapped in electric warmers and these ensure that the temperatures are maintained, even during the minute or so after the blankets have been removed and they wait for the green flag. But the problem is that, during the subsequent parade lap, the pressures and temperatures drop due to the fact that you are not running quickly enough to generate sufficient heat in the rubber. And, as Senna had pointed out, this business of running the Porsche pace car in Japan only made matters worse.

During the first few laps of the race, therefore, the car does not handle particularly well until the heat gets back into the tyres and the pressures come up. And at Imola, the problem was compounded when they had to do five laps behind the safety car. Certainly, Hill's car was more difficult to drive than usual during those first few laps after the restart.

He recalled: 'To be honest, I hadn't helped matters by messing up the restart slightly when the safety car pulled off. It so happened that, on the two occasions when the safety car had been used in the past, I had been leading. The trick is to drop back and give yourself a free run once the car disappears, but when you are in traffic, as I was at Imola, it is not possible to see exactly where the safety car is. It is best to stick with the guys in front but, in this instance, I had dropped back too much and when Ayrton and Michael took off at the restart, I was already about five seconds behind.

'But I had learned an important lesson. At Imola, there is a tight chicane just before the start/finish straight. When I slowed for the chicane, the brakes and the tyres were cold. I locked up my left front wheel and, for a terrible moment, I thought I was going to slide off the road before I had even started the first flying lap. That alerted me to the problem caused by the five slow laps behind the official car.'

Hill spent the first lap trying to cope with the car and concentrating on catching Gerhard Berger's Ferrari ahead of him in third place. He could see up ahead that Senna was leading Schumacher and they were quite close. There is no question that Senna, despite not wanting to race in the aftermath of Ratzenberger's death, was still highly motivated to beat Schumacher and was finding it frustrating not to be pulling away during those first few laps.

When Hill came through Tamburello for the second time, there was dust and debris and a car going sideways across the grass. He could see that it was Senna and said: 'At the time, I was busy dodging wheels and a nose wing that was flying through the air. I was pretty occupied as I went by but, once I'd got past the scene of the accident, I was concerned for Senna's safety. It had obviously been a very big shunt; you don't have a small one on that corner. My initial thoughts were that Ayrton and Michael had tangled and one of them had been pushed off.'

The race had been stopped and the rest of the cars pulled up at the pit lane entrance. Everyone was asking about what had happened but they had no information. One report suggested Senna had been moving. Then they said he was out of the car. But, either way, it was very possible that he was seriously hurt.

Hill was anxious to find out precisely what had taken place, and why. He went over to Michael Schumacher and asked him what he had seen. He explained that Senna's car had been bottoming a lot and he'd almost lost it at Tamburello on the previous lap. In his opinion, the same thing had happened again but this time Senna didn't catch it and went off. Hill asked Schumacher if he had seen any hint of trouble, perhaps with the suspension, or the tyres; something like that. He said he hadn't seen any problems at all.

'I took all of that on board,' recalled Hill, 'and made a note to be careful in the early stages when the tyre pressures might be low and perhaps the car is bottoming too much. But I still knew nothing about Ayrton's condition.' It is one of the less savoury aspects of motor racing that it is not considered to be a good idea to tell the whole truth at the time of an accident, in order to get the show over with and send people home none the wiser. Slowly, however, word trickled through that Ayrton's condition was quite serious.

'I just couldn't believe that this was happening. I thought that perhaps he'd hurt himself badly and he would be out for a couple of races. That was as much as I knew; that was as much as I would allow myself to think. I tried to concentrate on the race and motivate myself with the thought that it was very important that I get a result for the team. There was nothing I could do about Ayrton. The only thing was to do my job to the best of my ability.

'Despite making a reasonable start, that plan was wrecked halfway round the first lap as I tried to take second place off Schumacher. He was trying to get past Gerhard Berger and I don't think he realized I was so close.'

Berger's Benetton chopped straight across in front of Hill and accidentally took a nose wing off. That meant a pit stop for a replacement and the task of rejoining at the back of the field. It sounds callous, perhaps, but Hill's thoughts were either 'Things just aren't going our way this year,' or 'My God, this just gets worse.'

'Throughout the race, I just kept thinking that this was a job which had to be done. Nothing more than that,' Hill said. 'Much as I felt like it, there was no way I was going to pull in because that would have been completely the wrong thing to do.

'The only answer was to try to better the situation the team found themselves in and get the best result I could. Looking at it coldly, it was what I was paid to do and that was about as much enjoyment as I got out of it. One point for sixth place was hardly brilliant. It was something after a climb from last place – but what value was that in the context of everything which had happened over the weekend?'

Hill was pretty shattered by the end of the race; mentally and physically exhausted and emotionally drained as well. He spoke to team boss Frank Williams who explained that Senna was not in good shape. Hill remembers that he just wanted to get away from the circuit, just get in the car and go. 'My wife Georgie and I could have had a lift in the helicopter if we wanted to wait,' he said, 'but I just wanted to leave as soon as possible.'

They did that, even though it meant sitting for ages in a traffic jam. They missed their first flight but it was the last thing on Hill's mind. He was only worried about how Senna was going to pull through. When Hill and his wife reached the airport a member of the Williams team was waiting to tell them that Senna was dead. Hill was devastated.

'I had briefly considered that as a possibility,' he said, 'but put the thought out of my mind by reflecting on what I had learned about his condition. I had been told that he had serious head injuries and it seemed likely to me that he might never drive again. But that's about as far as my thinking had gone. To learn that he was dead was like having someone turn off your power supply. I was completely shaken; totally shattered.'

In deep shock, Damon and Georgie Hill drove off and stopped at a restaurant where they sat down to think about it all. It was at this moment that Damon Hill seriously considered quitting. The look in his wife's eyes said it all. Two friends dead and another lucky to be alive. Damon had too much to lose. 'You ask yourself over and over again, "Is it worth it?"' he admitted. 'That's the bottom line at the end of a weekend like this; always the same question, "Is it worth it?"'

Never before had Hill been so traumatized by the dark side of motor racing – although in certain respects it was not a new sensation for him. He can still remember playing in the front room at home when the newsflash came through that Jim Clark had been killed. He knew that Clark was his father's friend and, when his mother came into the room, he could see she was shocked. 'I didn't really understand what had happened,' he said. 'But I knew it was bad.'

Throughout that period of Damon Hill's life there were occasions when his father had to go to the funerals of friends. It was a gradual introduction to the reality of motor sport, at a time when the safety standards were nothing like they are now. It was a rather macabre and sobering rite of passage and Hill remembers thinking, 'Hang on, why is Dad doing this? It doesn't make sense.'

And yet Graham Hill carried on, irrespective of the fears for his safety. He did not give up because of the accidents and he drove through what was probably one of the most dangerous periods of Grand Prix racing. The irony was, of course, that he did not actually die in a racing car. And that itself was something which Damon Hill had to cope with. Graham Hill raced cars, faced the obvious dangers and yet he died in an aeroplane. Where was the logic in that? It was part of the learning process where young Damon discovered that bad things happen in life, even if you don't put yourself at risk. Horrible things occur all the time.

He said: 'To me, it seems the real tragedy would be to stop doing something you enjoy. There is no reward without risk. James Hunt died of a heart attack and yet who is to say that he did not live more, cram more into his 46 years than most people manage in a lifetime? I don't pretend to know the answer.

'Probably the easiest thing to do is carry on and convince yourself that you're doing the right thing. So I forced myself as much as possible to think about giving up and doing something else. Nothing definite sprang to mind but I knew I could do all the things which I had been forced to abandon for the sake of motor racing: weekends off, skiing, more time with the children, see my friends more often; that sort of thing.

'And yet I knew that, since an early age, I had always wanted to challenge myself. I needed those punctuations in my life where I had to face up to a severe test and the fact is that few things can offer that sort of opportunity. There are times when I feel totally happy with myself. It may not last long. It might be for a few hours, it could even be for a full day but, quite often, it is only a matter of minutes after I've done something that I'm really proud of. But those moments are addictive. Once you've had one, you need them again and again.

'You subconsciously think of the time when you've had enough (maybe after the highest high) and will give up, completely fulfilled. Until then, you continue to risk all for that fleeting moment. It may be different for other drivers. In fact, I can't begin to know how people such as Philippe Streiff and Martin Donnelly, put out of racing through serious injury, must feel. How much would they give to get back into a racing car? Or are they simply happy to be alive? It is not the sort of question you can put to them but it is something you need to ask yourself.'

There was almost too much time for Damon Hill to think about everything during the days which followed the 1994 San Marino Grand Prix. Ratzenberger and Senna were gone forever. It was like a nightmare but suddenly waking reality would hit Hill like a sledge-hammer. He deliberately chose not to watch television or look at newspapers the following day. He did not see the video of the accident until Tuesday, by which time he had decided that he really ought to find out what had happened. Then Hill learned that Senna's funeral would take place in São Paulo, and the healing process began.

The last thing Hill wanted at that point was to go to Brazil; given the choice, he would have gone away with his family and cut himself off until it was all over. He was not a close friend of Ayrton Senna because he had only really known him for a few months. But the fact was that he had to face certain things: Hill had to find how and why Senna had crashed and it was important to show his loyalty as his team-mate. He knew he had to go to the funeral and he's glad now that he did. 'I discovered just how much Ayrton meant to Brazil,' Hill said. 'The funeral was almost presidential; quite extraordinary. Thousands of people lined the streets and many ran alongside the cortege.

'It was a very long way and I saw one person run almost the full distance before falling into a hedge with exhaustion. There was a 21-gun salute carried out with great military precision, a fly-past, and a number of dignitaries, including the president of Argentina and the Japanese ambassador. Ayrton's family had requested that the drivers present escort the coffin as far as they could to the graveside, where there was a rifle salute.

'Overhead were four or five helicopters; it was a television spectacular of sorts but I couldn't hear any of the service because of the racket from above. I thought it rather sad that the family couldn't be left in peace during those final minutes. The furore over why he crashed was still raging in the media but, even though I was a member of the team, I was not aware of any animosity. In fact, it seemed to me quite the opposite.

'I was touched, particularly by the children who would have grown up knowing nothing but the success which Ayrton Senna brought to Brazil. It was obviously very difficult for them to understand what had happened to their hero. I remember being approached for my autograph by two fans as I left the hotel to go to the funeral. They said that Brazil would be watching me now – and that just choked me with emotion

'I suddenly realized that they loved motor racing and, because Ayrton had chosen Williams as his team, it had become their team as well. It was not that I was stepping into Ayrton's shoes or anything like that; it was just that Williams had become a part of their life and, by association, I was a part of it too. I thought it was a truly generous thing for them to say. All this was a lot for me to take on board.'

Hill had been looking forward to racing under the protective umbrella of Ayrton Senna. If he came second to Senna in a race then he could say he had done a good job – provided Senna wasn't too far ahead. But suddenly Hill was discovering the kind of responsibility Senna had been carrying all these years. He had been expected to win all the time.

'Being this person Ayrton Senna must have been a burden even if he did choose to carry it in the first place. In the short time that we had worked together, I had come to understand that he was a pretty special driver, an instinctive driver,' Hill added. 'If you gave him a car which wasn't quite perfect, he could still make it go very quickly; in fact, I don't think he knew any other way.

'I remember being intrigued by the way he would describe how the car handled. He would put his hands up in front of his face as if he was looking through the steering wheel, almost as if he was aiming the car. He had a very, very good ability to recall sensations and talk about the car repeatedly so that the engineer understood exactly what he was trying to say. It was in abstract terms. He wouldn't say the rollbar was too stiff. He would talk about sensations; refer to the road doing this or such and such a corner doing that, things I didn't even consider. He seemed to be able to see in minute detail exactly how the road changed.'

If a car was incapable of winning, Ayrton Senna could make it win. In the Brazilian Grand Prix, a few weeks before Imola, Senna had a car which was a bit off the pace of Schumacher's Benetton. Yet he was able to stay with the German and Hill was astounded that Senna had been able to do that with a car which, if it was anything like his, simply wasn't handling.

At one stage they were about to lap Hill. Schumacher came through and Hill thought he had better get out of Senna's way. But, almost before he had taken the decision, Senna dived past him and nearly went off. He was heading towards the grass and just managed to slither through. He had completely messed up the corner but, to him, the important thing was to get by; he wasn't going to lose any time hanging around waiting for Hill.

'It was as if he was being sucked towards the end of the race; as if you had attached one end of an elastic band to the start line and

wound the rest up for the number of laps – and then just let him go,'
recalled Hill. 'His desire to win was simply overwhelming. And
judging by the remarkable scenes at his funeral, he was doing it for a
nation he loved, a nation which loved him.'

By the time Hill returned home, the shock of Imola had worn off.
The incredible peace and warmth of Senna's funeral soothed even
the deepest emotional and mental wounds sustained during
Formula One's blackest weekend. And unexpectedly, for Hill
anyway, Senna's much publicized and personally professed faith in
God was proving the best healer of all. Hill was not a believer but on
the flight home he could not help thinking that Ayrton Senna is in
the heaven he so deeply believed in. That was healing enough, even
for a so-called atheist.

# 16

# Wheel of Life

*When men get hurt in the pursuit of glory it provides a huge thrill.
Of course, no one likes to see pain and suffering but the harsh reality
is that if Formula One was totally predictable in that accidents or
near misses did not happen then the sport would not be so popular.*

JACQUES VILLENEUVE

For someone who claims he is not afraid of death, Jacques
Villeneuve was pretty badly shaken by the infamous Molson Indy
tragedy in the summer of 1996. There is little that really scares
Villeneuve, but the former Indycar champion was nevertheless
deeply troubled by the terrible accident during the annual Toronto
race that killed two men he knew.

When 31-year-old driver Jeff Krosnoff of LaCanada, California,
and track marshal Gary Arvin of Calgary died, Villeneuve searched
his soul. Perhaps for the first time since his father Gilles lost his life
in a motor racing accident, the young Canadian weighed up the cost
of taking such huge risks in the high-speed pursuit of fame and
fortune. And, no matter how hard he tried, he could not shake off
the awful realization that absolutely no one escapes their own
mortality, not even the fastest men on earth. The image of the
smashed and twisted corpses of Krosnoff and Arvin hammered this
truth home with a vengeance.

The accident that killed these two people instantly was seen
countless times on television broadcasts. What happened is simply
this: one second, three drivers – Krosnoff, Andre Ribeiro and Stefan
Johansson – were speeding along at approximately 250 mph. The next,
one car became airborne, smashing into a catch fence separating

spectators and course workers from the racing surface. The car disintegrated as it hit the track, breaking into many pieces. The driver's monocoque cockpit, theoretically impenetrable, was badly damaged. Krosnoff and Arvin were dead instantly.

Jeff Krosnoff was one of the upcoming stars of Indycar. An experienced racer, coming into Indy from five years in the Japanese Formula 3000 series and three Le Mans 24-hour races (2nd overall 1994). He began a successful racing career in 1983 and had graduated from UCLA with a degree in psychology in 1987. He was having a difficult year in 1996, driving in an uncompetitive car powered by rookie Indy engine maker Toyota.

The accident occurred on the 92nd lap out of 95, just after the start-finish line, at the fastest section of the track. The track was an 11-turn temporary street circuit. Coming down the straight at over 180 mph, Krosnoff made wheel-to-wheel contact with Stefan Johansson, flipping his car into the air. It went airborne into a steel catch fence.

The car spun along the fence, disintegrating as it went. The impact deflected the fence back far enough for the car to hit a tree behind the fence. The car continued along the fence, impacting a concrete light pole on the outside of the catch fence, although protected by a concrete barrier at track level. Krosnoff was killed instantly upon impact with the light pole, the front of the car shearing off and exposing his legs as it disintegrated. The engine and transmission continued on past the incident and landed on another competitor, Emerson Fittipaldi, who escaped injury.

Several spectators were hit with flying debris and a track corner worker, Gary Arvin, was killed. The race was halted as the accident was so severe and so close to the designated race end. The other damaged cars came to rest 90 metres away, their drivers unhurt. The race instantly went to a full-course yellow alert, with the pace car sent out to pick up the race leader, Adrian Fernandez of Mexico. The pace car led the field once through the carnage and then, the next time past the start-finish line, the chequered flag was waved along with a red flag, the motor racing signal of grave danger, which ended the race two laps early.

The cars stopped in a single-file line along Lake Shore Boulevard, short of where medical personnel were working to help Krosnoff and Arvin. The CART safety team was on site quickly but could do little to revive Krosnoff who had suffered massive head, chest and skeletal injuries in the impact. He was pronounced dead on arrival at hospital.

The coroner's report into the accident directed blame at no individuals or organizations, but outlined a set of recommendations aimed at reducing the impact of a similar accident in the future. These recommendations included 'additional debris fencing on barriers in designated locations around the track'. The recommendation of debris fencing 'on' the barriers would avoid the possibility of an object such as the light pole being hit by an airborne car.

The coroner recommended that the corner workers should be protected behind safety fencing in specially designed safety cutouts. This would have prevented the death of Gary Arvin, who was hit either by debris or by the car itself, the Coroner being unable to establish the precise cause of his death. One thing is certain, though; Arvin's fate shocked Molson and left a dark cloud over the sport in Canada.

If a race track or speedway goes quiet when it's not supposed to, there is always somehow a sense of foreboding. Everyone talks optimistically about how everything will probably be okay, and how their thoughts and prayers are with the people who are injured, but there are no smiles and the look deep within their eyes betrays any outward levity. The scream of engines becomes a deathly whisper and the odour of oil and methanol no longer a smell that stimulates good memories; people who watched Krosnoff and Arvin die will go to other races and inhale oil and methanol but only taste death.

For Jacques Villeneuve, the awful tragedy of the July '96 Molson Indy made him realize just how lucky he had been during his own Indycar career. That summer when motor racing killed Krosnoff and Arvin, Villeneuve had already switched to Formula One, but it could have been so different had fate twisted the other way two years earlier. Then Villeneuve was lucky to be alive after being involved in a bad crash during the 1994 Indycar World Series. It happened at the Phoenix International Raceway on Sunday 10 April – on the infamous oval circuit that is dubbed 'the world's fastest one-mile oval'; an amphitheatre amid the cacti and a place which had injured Nigel Mansell in 1993 on his oval debut, causing him to crash and to watch the race from his hospital bed after damaging his lower back.

Now there is no doubt in anybody's mind that this is a very serious business, one that becomes deadly in the blink of an eye. But back then, at the time of his 23rd birthday, and right up until the death of Krosnoff and Arvin, Villeneuve had never once allowed any sign of fear or trepidation to creep into his thinking. He just shut it out – dismissed it even – with a nonchalant shrug of his shoulders. 'Hey, if it happens, it happens,' he would say, referring to the possibility of death from his chosen game.

The race at the Phoenix International Raceway was traumatic for everyone who was there – except for Villeneuve himself who, according to eyewitnesses, was not only able to survive and walk away from the carnage but did so as if he had been out for a Sunday stroll, instead of involved in a massive accident in which he carved another driver's vehicle in half. *Autosport* reported that a 'wild multi-car accident' took place, triggered by Hiro Matsuhita in a Simon-Lolo clipping wheels with Teo Fabi's Hall-Reynard on turn three as Fabi tried to lap the Japanese driver. The leaders were running directly behind this pair and as Fabi and Matsuhita's cars spun into the retaining wall, Tracy, in a Penske, found himself with nowhere to go. He was taken into the wall by Matsuhita's car, which was then hit by Villeneuve. The young Canadian's Reynard T-boned Matsuhita's car, and was then in turn hit by Dobson. It was remarkable that Villeneuve escaped uninjured from his wrecked Reynard, which ended up part way down the pit lane.

It was a colossal accident and a near miracle that Villeneuve and Matsuhita were not killed. Villeneuve appeared not to notice any need to slow down despite the fact that the yellow warning flags were being waved and Mario Andretti was slowing ahead of him. Observers said Villeneuve ploughed into the accident and only braked a few feet before the impact. Matsuhita's car was smashed apart, but the driver escaped with only a dislocated shoulder. Villeneuve was not even dazed. Later that night he settled down to read a J. R. R. Tolkien book as though nothing had happened. It is his way of escaping reality and, to a certain extent, mortality, although there are times when even the pages of a fantasy book fail to rescue Villeneuve from the harsh facts of life.

The magic kingdoms of writers such as Tolkien allow Villeneuve to escape, if only for a short while, the intensity of motor racing and he has been inhabiting such private worlds from the age of 10, when he would head off alone down the ski slopes of Quebec. His Formula One career, which began in March 1996 and embraced a world championship in only his second season, has been another journey into solitude, even though Villeneuve has become one of the most celebrated stars of Grand Prix racing. Behind the cool and crazy exterior is a complex, deep thinking, spiritual human being who believes in faith and destination and, after several close shaves with death, has come to accept that only so much of that lies in his own hands.

After making his Formula One debut, at the Albert Park circuit in Melbourne on 10 March 1996, Villeneuve – the winner of the 1995 Indianapolis 500, the most prestigious race in America – faced up to the reality of trying to leave his own imprint on a sport where the dead forever haunt the living. As son of a famous but departed father, Jacques Villeneuve would not only have to win the world championship but would have to push himself beyond the limits of human endurance and tolerance in doing so. Gilles Villeneuve lived and died on the edge and Jacques is tempting the same fate, as do all men who drive racing cars. 'I'm not afraid of death,' he said. 'It's natural. You are born and then you die. Death is part of the wheel of life. There is no point in making it come quicker on purpose, but in this job the chances are it might. Racing is very dangerous. There is always that risk and this edge of pushing yourself, and always pushing it more. Death is always on the agenda.'

A psychologist might wonder why he would want to climb into the sort of contraption that killed his father in Belgium in 1982. Whatever that did to Jacques – he was 11 at the time, and wrote poems about his father on the way home for the funeral – he has navigated his own path through life since, and says he rarely looks in the great rear-view mirror of memory. The psychologist might speculate that Villeneuve is pursuing the ghost of his father in the fastest conveyance available. Such a simplification ignores the son's own development through an idyllic childhood that was lived outdoors, and forever dusted with the snow of Canadian winters.

After answering thousands of questions about the legacy of his father's death, he has tired of talking about the co-driver whom people imagine he races with. 'It's a morbid fascination for some,' he says. 'But it's not how it is for me. I'm not preoccupied with my father's death or my own fate. I love racing, I love life, and I love taking risks. What's wrong with that?'

They called him 'Mr Smiley' in the Williams camp, before he moved to British American Racing at the end of the 1998 Grand Prix season, because he is seldom worn down by the incessant demands of the Formula One circus. A soft glitter fills those eyes when he recalls his early years. 'If you went on the slopes with your skis at 10 years of age, there would be no parents having an eye on you to see whether you were going to hurt yourself. In Quebec on holidays I would hop on my motocross and go off through the woods. If anything happened to me nobody would have known. That was a good way to grow up, because it made me what I am today.'

Jacques Villeneuve was only 10 when his father failed to come home from work that sunny May afternoon 17 years ago. The world mourned the passing of a legend; the boy was left to cope with the death of a father. 'I can't remember too much,' says the adult Jacques, his ice-blue eyes showing no sign of emotion. 'I don't know if I have buried that day or if it's just too far away. I don't have a lot of memories of my father. He was never at home – he was always racing, testing, playing with his boat or whatever.'

More than any other sport, motor racing makes enormous demands on the families of the drivers whom the public see only as heroes, blithely ignoring the less glamorous side of their lives as husbands and fathers. Though Jacques Villeneuve was raised in luxury in Monte Carlo and educated in Switzerland, although he became an Olympic-standard skier and although he was showered with go-karts, snowmobiles and motocross bikes by his father, he was essentially brought up by his mother Joann. He cannot, for instance, ever remember losing to his father at his boyhood passion, Scalextric. 'Yes, I always won. I always played by myself, so I always won.'

Recalling Jacques' relationship with his father, Joann Villeneuve talked of the nervous headaches and problems at school the young Jacques experienced. She said: 'Gilles was very demanding – he wanted his son to be more than perfect. I didn't have any problems with Jacques. He would sit calmly at the table and not drop his glass of milk. But when Gilles was there he would drop the glass of milk. He would get very nervous just trying so hard to please his father.'

If any psychological scar tissue remains, Villeneuve junior is too canny, too respectful of his father's memory to allow a stranger close enough to see the marks of resentment. When asked if he would have any hesitation about starting a family while still racing, he replies with feeling: 'Of course not. It's stupid, but you never believe you will hurt yourself. I certainly wouldn't mind having children, because if I weren't driving a racing car I would be doing something even crazier. It was hard to accept my father was never coming back, but it has not been something that destroyed my life. It didn't disturb me too much.'

Unlike Damon Hill, who followed his father's chosen career only after much soul-searching, Jacques Villeneuve has always accepted what destiny had planned for him. 'I grew up in the pits of Monaco and Monza and just sort of knew I was always going to be a racer. There was no flash of lightning or crack of thunder from the heavens. It's what I was born to do. Simple as that. Maybe motor racing is in the genes, but when you grow up in a family like mine then this is the only world you ever know.'

The father would have fully empathized with his son's infatuation with speed, his love of 'living on the edge' as he describes it, but what of Joann Villeneuve, who was only 31 when motor racing made a widow of her? Jacques said: 'She was completely supportive. She wasn't entirely happy, of course, because she'd lost a husband and she doesn't want to see her son get hurt. But my mother had been with my father since she was 17 when he was racing snowmobiles, so this was her world, too. She has always known I was going to race. I guess she's known it from the moment I was born.'

The son may have inherited the father's fascination with speed, danger and excitement, but he was also born with a measure of restraint, patience and self-preservation. Instead of simply putting his foot to the floor, as Gilles Villeneuve most certainly would have done, Jacques Villeneuve applied the brakes to his natural instincts.

His famous victory in the 1995 Indianapolis 500 is a case in point. Penalized two laps (a daunting five miles which left him 32nd and last) after inadvertently overtaking the pace car while crash debris was being removed from the circuit, Villeneuve plotted his moves like a chess player. Gradually weaving his way through the field with a series of deft overtaking manoeuvres, he finally took the lead on lap 127.

'I wouldn't have believed it possible. He came from over the horizon,' said Brazilian virtuoso Emerson Fittipaldi, who has raced against both father and son. 'He is different from Gilles, yet he is the same. Gilles is remembered as the fastest driver in history. Jacques, I think, can be as fast. He is very special.'

Something special, indeed. Not just because he was the youngest-ever Indycar Series champion at the age of 24. Not just because he can charm sponsors in fluent English, French and Italian (plus an everyday knowledge of Japanese). Not just because he is roguishly handsome, discreetly intelligent and joyously unpretentious. And not because he is the son of a god. No, Jacques Villeneuve is special because, like his father, death holds no fear for him – even though he doesn't believe in life after death, at least the Christian version.

'I'm not sure what happens to a person after they die,' he says. 'I've got an open mind about stuff like that. I believe in God, or at least some greater power than mankind, and I don't believe that we are alone in this universe. There is a greater purpose to our existence than purely our own selfish, material needs. I suppose when you live on the edge, in terms of facing danger and the possibility of death from your chosen profession, you are perhaps more in touch with your spiritual side. I love life, I love what I do, but I know there is more to life than fame and fortune. I've heard people say that my father had some kind of death wish, that he took too many risks, was reckless etc. But I know one thing, he loved life and lived it to the full.'

Gilles Villeneuve achieved a mere six victories in 67 races before he was killed during practice for the 1982 Belgian Grand Prix at Zolder, yet the French-Canadian, just 32 when he died, was idolized as no other driver before or since.

Villeneuve senior was reckless. He drove like there was no tomorrow and his number 27 Ferrari, a notoriously uncompetitive tank for much of his tragically brief career, was all over the place. If Villeneuve had been at the back of the grid in a clapped-out banger, he would have driven like a man possessed in an attempt to overtake every car in front of him. 'He did everything in life at 200 mph,' recalled close friend and long-time rival Patrick Tambay at the funeral. 'Everything – skiing, racing his speedboat, playing backgammon.'

Gilles Villeneuve was the 71st driver to be handed the keys of a Formula One Ferrari and none of his predecessors – not even Alberto Ascari, Mike Hawthorn or Niki Lauda – was so beloved by the fearsome Il Commandatore. 'I like to think Ferrari can build drivers as well as cars,' commented Enzo Ferrari when questioned about the advisability of hiring this unknown novice from Quebec. 'Some people say Villeneuve is crazy. I say, "Let's try him".' The old man came to look upon Villeneuve as a son, even permitting the young daredevil to crack a rare joke at the boss's expense during the celebration party following the number 27 Ferrari's victory at Monaco in 1981.

'I wish the Pope would make you a Cardinal,' said Villeneuve. 'And why is that?' came the deceptively soft reply. 'Because then we would only have to kiss your ring ...' A cold silence descended upon the gathering in Monte Carlo's Hermitage Hotel. Then, after what seemed an eternity, Enzo Ferrari roared with laughter. Gilles had pulled off another unlikely triumph.

In *Villeneuve* (Collins Willow, 1997), a definitive biography by the Canadian sportswriter Gerald Donaldson, a gridful of motor racing personalities are lined up to offer their tributes:

*Gilles was someone I took a great liking to. I liked everything about him. He was the craziest devil I ever came across in Formula One.*

NIKI LAUDA

*He was somewhat crazy, but surely a phenomenon. He was able to do things nobody else could do.*

NELSON PIQUET

*Everyone agrees that Gilles was always risking more than any other driver. That was how he made his career.*

EDDIE CHEEVER

*The crowds loved him because, of all the men out there, he was so clearly working without a safety net. His approach to motor racing was possibly too passionate to ever bring him a world championship, but it explains why he was worshipped like no other driver.*

FORMULA ONE JOURNALIST NIGEL ROEBUCK

The magic of the Villeneuve name is something that just follows Jacques around, like the journalists and the fans who pursue his actions and thoughts to the very edge of psychosis. But 'the edge' is something Villeneuve talks about a lot. 'The rush' too. The intoxication of downhill skiing was leading him ever closer to a life on the professional circuit, but turned out to be a mild tingle compared to the thrills of the pit lanes. 'If you start from pole, cruise around and end up winning, it's boring,' he says. 'If you have to fight for it, then it becomes entertaining. Danger is entertaining.'

And, with morbid regret, so is death. 'Yes, there is no denying that,' Villeneuve admits. 'Part of the thrill of motor racing for the fans and the media is the possibility that something bad could happen. It's the same reason why boxing is so popular. When men get hurt in the pursuit of glory it provides a huge thrill. Of course, no one likes to see pain and suffering but the truth is, if Formula One was totally predictable in that accidents or near misses did not happen then the sport would not be so popular.'

## 17

# Happy Jacques

*The more dangerous it is, the more fun you get out of it. But there is a point when acceptable danger becomes the unacceptable risk. There is no victory in death.*

GILLES VILLENEUVE

You can deny the truth and hide from it. You can cheat it and ignore it. You can run from it, be afraid of it, and despise it. You can do many things with the truth but you can't escape it. The truth always finds you in the end. It rides shotgun with conscience in the carriage of your best dreams and worst nightmares. Like a bloodhound following the strongest scent it tracks your every move across the wide-open kaleidoscope of life. And like the brightest searchlight penetrates the deepest, darkest hiding place. The truth is an omnipotent force. It detects you and wakes you. It checks you and troubles you. It condemns, vindicates and liberates. The truth is all things to all people.

The truth about Gilles Villeneuve is that he was addicted to danger. He took unacceptable risks he had no right to take. Why? Because he had a wife and young son and that should have been reason enough to kick his deadly habit. I am not condemning Gilles Villeneuve because for me he is the greatest racing driver of all time, even better than Senna and Clark and they raced at extremes of danger and speed. But Gilles Villeneuve performed on the most outward edge of the rim between common sense and insanity. He really did work without a safety net and that is why motor racing fans loved him so much.

Of course, he had great hands, a brilliant racing mind and a competitive spirit that never conceded defeat until the day he died.

Even then I doubt it was broken. Lost maybe, but not broken. But he raced with such wild abandon and with total disregard for the consequences of his actions. He had no fear even though he knew his life would probably end prematurely in some terrible smash. When the end came for Gilles Villeneuve he wasn't running or hiding from the truth. He was hurtling straight at it, at blistering speed.

For this reason, more than any other, Jacques Villeneuve is proud of his father. 'He was happiest on the edge,' Jacques said. 'And I admire him for that. My father was a man of strong conviction. He wanted to race, he loved to drive very fast and take chances other drivers would not take. He died doing what he loved the most. He hadn't a problem with that. He could not have lived a lie, he was too honest to do that.'

Many people accuse Jacques of having the same addiction to danger as his father and Villeneuve junior admits he too is happiest on the edge, although he insisted: 'But that doesn't mean I'm playing with death. Yeah, right on the edge, always pushing it. Knowing where your boundaries are and trying to get better so you can push these boundaries. Knowing you almost lost it, but managed to keep it going where other guys wouldn't. That brings a big smile.'

And like father, like son … Jacques knows no fear. 'The danger never frightens me,' he added. 'Sometimes you get moments where your heart starts beating very hard and it hurts inside – like if you try to take a corner flat out and you just miss it by a little bit. It's not fear – I don't know what it is – maybe you could call it an apprehension, but it gives you a special feeling.'

These days, after spending 12 years experiencing much of what his father did, Villeneuve has a fatalistic view of his bereavement. 'One day or another he would have died doing something crazy. He died doing what he loved doing. It is the normal cycle of life.

'I am really proud of my father and no matter how much success I have as a driver it will never diminish his accomplishments or what his memory means to Formula One fans. Because of my father I was born into a racing environment and it felt like a normal world to me. After he was killed, in 1982, I became interested in speed for myself.

'I was only 11 years old then and I loved going fast on skis or on a motocross bike and soon I wanted to race cars. But I've never wanted to follow in his footsteps. That's not the reason I'm doing it. I'm racing for myself.'

His father's reputation certainly helped Jacques Villeneuve to get his racing career started but it also put a lot more pressure on the young French-Canadian because people compared them all the time and wanted Jacques to live up to the family name. 'From my first race, everyone knew who I was and they were expecting me to win,' he said.

Maybe those expectations and that extra pressure helped his progression as a driver because he had to work harder. 'I will never know, because that's the only way it's ever been,' he admitted. 'All I know for sure is that as a racing driver I've never been content to accept anything less than being able to challenge to win.'

As for death itself, Jacques Villeneuve recognizes the risk – having lost his father and his friend Roland Ratzenberger in Formula One – but is very philosophical about it. He insists, 'I've never looked at anything and thought, "that's dangerous", in a way that keeps me away from it. The danger itself is something you calculate anyway, because you're the one controlling your medium.' For that reason, he's not interested in so-called dangerous sports like bungee jumping. 'I don't like the idea, because you just jump and you have no control.'

That's one way of looking at it, but Jacques Villeneuve has another theory and one that his father would have embraced whole-heartedly. This other angle is that there is now little difference between motor racing and bungee jumping at all. Because of new safety regulations, notably those regulating tyre and chassis design, racing speeds are destined to remain significantly lower with fewer thrills and spills. The risk element has diminished and the dangers are nowhere near as real as in the days of Gilles Villeneuve. And that is not to Jacques' liking.

'Too much emphasis has been put on safety when it was already safe enough,' he said. 'I'm not saying it should be more dangerous, just that there should always be a little voice saying "Don't make a mistake". There isn't that apprehension to overcome now, which is a shame. It's like bungee jumpers, I guess. They're scared to jump; yet they know nothing can happen. I'm not interested in that: you don't control anything.'

The new safety regulations will save lives in Formula One but driving at the edge may never be the same again. 'Knowing you're on that razor's edge, at the very limit, and controlling it, is the greatest feeling,' he added. 'But you don't get that sensation so much when there is so much emphasis put on safety. I love the fighting, the competition. I need it – the excitement of trying to beat the opposition. But I also need the danger. I need to be in that situation where I know one mistake could kill me.'

That is an extreme statement, especially coming from someone whose father was killed by the same addiction to danger. Even more surprising, disturbing even, is Jacques Villeneuve's opposition to new safety regulations even though his close friend Roland Ratzenberger voiced his concern about safety in Formula One only days before he died following his accident during qualifying for the 1994 San Marino Grand Prix.

The real irony of all this is that on one occasion Jacques Villeneuve would probably have been killed along with his father, Ratzenberger and the rest, had it not been for improved safety standards in the sport. This fact is not lost on Villeneuve, although he pays it little attention. In his mind, he is still alive because the gods of motor racing smiled on him instead of requesting the pleasure of his company. Fate may not be so kind next time.

His lucky escape happened 15 years after Gilles Villeneuve was killed in 1982 at Zolder. Jacques Villeneuve emerged from the wreckage of his Williams Meccachrome's 185 mph crash at Raidillon with nothing worse than a bruised knee and a relieved grin. His survival was a symbol of Formula One's successful progress in improving safety standards and saving lives.

In seasons past, with inferior car and circuit standards, the defending world champion would almost certainly have been seriously injured, at least. His shunt at the top of the hill, as he accelerated out of the fearsome Eau Rouge corner below, was the most alarming of the 1997 Grand Prix season, if less spectacular than the sight of Alexander Wurz barrel-rolling his Benetton on the opening lap of the Canadian Grand Prix.

The crumpled wreckage of his car tells its own story. Eight years ago, in a similar accident, Alessandro Zanardi was badly hurt when he lost control of his Lotus Ford at the same place. The Italian, who later became Indycar champion, suffered chronic concussion and neck injuries. In 1985 Stefan Bellof was killed at Eau Rouge during the 1,000 Kilometres de Spa event when he tried to overtake.

'Happy' Jacques Villeneuve limped upstairs in the Williams motorhome. He had a stiff neck and a sore back. He slumped in a chair and closed his eyes for a moment. Maybe he thought of his father or his friend Roland Ratzenberger or maybe nothing at all. One thing is certain, though, it wasn't long before the shock wore off and he started to enjoy the strangely pleasant sensation of cheating death.

'That was a big one,' said Villeneuve. 'Easily the biggest in my Formula One career and one of the biggest I have ever had. I had some big ones in my time in America in oval racing, but that was as big as any of them. It was the best crash of my F1 career. When I knew I had lost it, I thought "This is going to hurt". It did. I was glad to get out of it.

'I like to drive on the edge and I was definitely on the edge in that one. I was over 290 kph at the apex of Eau Rouge and I was trying to do it all flat. I just lost it. Plain and simple. It was a little scary but I would do it again.'

Perhaps Villeneuve is not in touch with reality. Maybe he is so addicted to danger that reality is an illusion, a trick of the mind. In his mind, after his accident, he had simply had some fun and he revelled in the excitement with all the surreal enthusiasm of a child. For him the potentially fatal accident had been real fun, the kind that kills you when it stops becoming a joke; like poking a cobra with a stick. Only a fool or a madman would do that – someone who doesn't care if they get struck in the face by an angry, belting venomous snake. Or perhaps someone with a naïve understanding of consequence.

Villeneuve lost control of his car on the fastest section of the circuit other drivers call 'the only real track we've got left'. It is a daunting stretch, which rises up towards the clouds on the skyline of the Ardennes forests through which the Spa-Francorchamps snakes and dips for 4.329 miles.

Thoughts of slowing came late. The deep black scars of rubber from his belated braking demonstrated this, before his car plunged across a short gravel trap and spun backwards into the tyres which protected the steel barriers. The back end, missing the rear wing and engine covers, was severely damaged.

Villeneuve climbed out of the wreckage and smiled but beneath the cool, rather nonchalant exterior, there was anger. Anger because he had lost control; beaten by the twisting speed of Raidillon. Anger because, probably, Gilles Villeneuve would not have been.

Although he won't admit it, Jacques Villeneuve is forever pursuing the glorious, shimmering ghost Ferrari of his father. The son of a legend is, perhaps, afraid to be a mere mortal. Even though the true fragility and vulnerability of Gilles Villeneuve, and every other speed king who dared to take death by the horns and died grappling with danger, was brutally exposed. Jacques must be aware that the killing machine and the pleasure machine are one and the same.

Motor racing is one of the few sports where team-mates compete against each other – rather than everyone else – and death or serious injury is an acceptable downside. It is also one of the few sports where the legacy of death is blind motivation.

Villeneuve once said of his father: 'Even if I won five world championships I wouldn't attain his level.' But he would not be scorching round race tracks if he thought he would become just a footnote to the Gilles Villeneuve obituary. Jacques did not simply inherit his father's obsession with danger and speed and his courage and skill, he absorbed the full energy of Gilles Villeneuve's soul; he became a carrier, infected with glorious self-destruction.

Jacques played with a model Ferrari while his dad drove the real thing, and drew pictures of cars on the flight back to Canada as they prepared to bury the legend. Now he drives them himself, less for the abstract pleasure of winning titles than the euphoria of the chase. But there is more to his motivation than plain satisfaction. There is the fear of failure. The fear of not quite matching up to the powerful images of the daredevil who piloted Ferrari No. 27.

Maybe Villeneuve is driven by something else, a demon more powerful than the one that pushed his father to the edge and beyond. This is the real fear of failure. It is the definitive mental torture for a sportsman and beating it, winning the fight with yourself, is the ultimate personal victory. But what if the fight is with a memory or a deep psychological trauma? What if it is a fight which cannot be won?

In interviews with *Esquire* magazine and the *Montreal Gazette* before the start of the 1999 Formula One season, Villeneuve, preparing for his Grand Prix debut with new team British American Racing, admitted to covering up much of the anguish and 'sometimes fighting a lonely, personal battle to be myself'.

Immediately after Gilles Villeneuve died Jacques coped badly. It was the Beau Soleil school in Villars, on the side of a Swiss mountain, that helped him come to terms with the reality of his terrible loss. He shared his schooldays there with Charlotte Gainsbourg, daughter of Serge, and hung out with President Mobutu's son. For Villeneuve, the effect ran deeper than that: 'In Monaco [where he was growing up] there was something wrong,' he told *Esquire*. 'I was a bit withdrawn after the death of my father; I was doing badly in school. As soon as I arrived here, I was freer somehow ... I started working properly, I skied a lot, played other sports. Also, I adore the mountains – that's how it was in Canada [where he was born]. I began to accept what happened to my father. I realized there was nothing anyone could have done to prevent his death.'

In Timothy Collins' book *The New Villeneuve* Jacques is quoted as saying: 'I am not racing because my father left too early and I have to carry the name and the tradition. I don't really care about tradition. I'm racing because I have fun and enjoy it.'

Several years later and Jacques Villeneuve embraces the same philosophy, but adds: 'In many ways I think all of life is good, or at least has the potential to be positive. The pain and suffering are not accidents. Pain and suffering were designed into this complex and intelligent life we live. They are here for a good reason.'

A Christian viewpoint might be that hard times are there to bring a person closer to God; humble a person, make them feel helpless, break down their artificial support systems and weaker ways of thinking. It is in weakness that trust and dependence on God comes to its full power. Villeneuve, however, does not see it like that. He is more comfortable with the philosophy of the old Chinese saying: 'Pain makes me think, thinking makes me wise and wisdom makes life endurable.'

'That makes more sense to me than accepting that man is vulnerable and only strong when fully dependent on God,' he said. 'We all have weaknesses and we all make mistakes and experience some form of pain and suffering, be it physical, mental, emotional or spiritual. When I accepted that the death of my father was just part of the wheel of life and that instead of making me weaker could make me stronger, a better person, I was released from a lot of the fear and the hurt. I also realized I could be fulfilled without necessarily winning all of the time. I don't strive like I used to.

'Striving is negative. It can burn you out, distort your judgement, and make you an angry, selfish individual. Striving takes the fun out of life. Life is meant to be fun and so is motor racing. My father raced because it was fun to him. It gave him enormous pleasure. Obviously he loved to win but if he didn't he was still a happy man.'

Gilles Villeneuve is remembered as one of the most charismatic drivers of his age, largely due to the fact that his enthusiasm for the sport was infectious. Gilles Villeneuve pursued his love of danger and speed with a burning passion; his ambition was fuelled by sheer pleasure.

But Formula One can squeeze that pleasure until drivers develop a permanent frown. 'Some have the weight of the world on their shoulders,' Villeneuve added. 'They are not happy, until they learn how to enjoy life again, and by enjoyment I don't only mean the pleasures money can buy. I'm talking about the simple things in life. The basic fulfilments of just being alive and being fortunate enough to do what you love the most. But sometimes you have to endure pain before you appreciate just how good life is.'

There is another old saying that goes something like this: 'The first element of virtue has to be endurance. Without endurance nothing will develop.' Villeneuve is not the only driver who had to learn the difference between striving and enduring. Michael Schumacher, the 1995 Formula One World Champion, is a case in point.

According to ITV reporter James Allen in his book *Michael Schumacher: The Quest For Redemption* (Partridge, 1999), when Mika Hakkinen became world champion at Suzuka at the end of the 1998 Formula One season, the first to congratulate him was a man in a Ferrari sweater and jeans, 'a man at peace with himself, beaten but upbeat, making a genuine expression of sporting congratulation to his conqueror'. It is Allen's contention that in that handshake, the Ferrari star 'had begun to find the redemption he had been searching for since Jerez'.

No one, especially Villeneuve, needs reminding of the collision that resulted in Schumacher becoming the first driver in history to be disqualified from the points table for unsportsmanlike driving. *Daily Telegraph* journalist Sarah Edworthy said that '[Schumacher's] mistake in 1997 was twofold: one, the cynical turn of the wheel in an attempt to cripple Villeneuve; two, the refusal to publicly accept blame for the incident'.

'No outsider is privy to the internal dialogue of a champion mourning his loss. Schumacher is often accused of being more like a robot than a human being and it was clear in the immediate aftermath of Jerez that he had attempted to park his error in the appropriate space and move on. The analysis had come later; too much later,' writes Allen.

From Argentina 1998 (a rude barging manoeuvre on Coulthard) to Canada (a flying exit from the pit lane that forced Frentzen off the track) to Spa (attempted fisticuffs with Coulthard) and finally to Suzuka, Schumacher learned to accept he might be at fault. He also learned how to enjoy motor racing again. 'I think there have been times during my career when I have strived for success instead of reaching for it,' Schumacher admitted. 'I am much more relaxed now, much more philosophical about the job I do, and life in general.

'I think existing in such an extreme environment puts you in touch with the things that really matter; honesty, communication, trust, a sense of making the most of each day. Life is too short to allow negative thoughts and actions to rule your life.'

Unlike Jacques Villeneuve's traumatic rite of passage from bereaved son of a legend to relatively happy-go-lucky champion Formula One driver, Michael Schumacher has enjoyed a smooth, shock-free rise to motor racing stardom, although he too has been deeply troubled, wounded even, by the extreme and ruthlessly unpredictable nature of the sport. There is one moment in particular he will never forget because it happened during the year he won the Formula One title.

For German fans, Schumacher was their country's first – and long overdue – world champion, 33 years after Wolfgang von Trips was killed at the wheel of his Ferrari in the Italian Grand Prix just as he seemed poised to grasp the title crown. Yet Schumacher's success in the 1994 battle for the title was not easy and straightforward, by any means.

To begin with, he believed that he would not have won the world championship at all had Ayrton Senna not crashed and suffered fatal injuries in San Marino. The young German was in Senna's mirrors when tragedy robbed Formula One of its supreme practitioner. The king was dead, the heir was on the throne prematurely, and dogged by self-doubt.

'It's the first time I have been confronted with death, and it was the worst time I had really in my life,' Schumacher said during a Channel 9 telecast of the Australian Grand Prix on 13 November 1994. 'And I wasn't sure if I was going to be the same racing driver as I was before, and I really had to go out in a test and try out. I had to find out whether I would sense danger at every corner, if I still could go to the limit, or if I couldn't.'

He could, and he went on to win the 1994 world championship, but even now, six years later, Schumacher is still occasionally haunted by the spectre of Senna's awful death. It is a deep anxiety that flutters from time to time and, for all his composure and ruthlessly efficient attitude, Schumacher is as vulnerable as the next man when it comes to facing the sobering truth of mortality. 'Some people make out like he is some kind of robot, an efficient machine with no feelings,' Michael's father Rolf once remarked. 'But let me tell you something. Whenever motor racing kills a driver, Michael hurts, is a little afraid maybe. Of course, they pay him well because of the danger, but even the richest man in the world cannot buy immunity from death. It is no respecter of fame or fortune.'

Schumacher's father was not wealthy. But he supported and encouraged his eldest son to start karting at a track in their home town. Just by coincidence, Germany's first world champion grew up not far from the family estate where the von Trips family had lived and the luckless Wolfgang had spent his childhood.

'Home was in Kerpen, near Cologne,' Schumacher said. 'My father was a builder, not a rich man; we went into motor racing in the cheapest possible way. That is, go-kart to start. I had the childhood of any other boy. Playing football, climbing trees, getting into a little trouble. Absolutely normal. Until one weekend, when I was maybe 11, I had to decide whether to take part in a judo competition or a go-kart race. I chose judo, came third, and I knew that was the wrong decision.

'Even then, racing was a hobby. I had no fantasies of GP racing. It was only when I was 20 and went to Mercedes in their young driver squad that I said "Hey, maybe this is what you do for a living." Only then.

'For me, it was never a target to be a Formula One driver. The financial point was not there to think about. If you have some parents that have the money, to put you in a Formula Ford or Two or whatever, where you can think about some developing and going on in the real motorsport world, then it's maybe different, but for me it was never the case, I was happy with what I did in go-kart. I earned enough money to live with it, and no, there was never real thought about any Formula thing.'

In 1984, Schumacher clinched the German junior kart championship and retained the title the following year. By 1987, he had won the German senior title, switched to cars in 1988 and then tackled the highly competitive German Formula Three championship the following year. He wound up third in the final points table behind Karl Wendlinger and Heinz-Harald Frentzen – and all three of them were recruited by Mercedes Benz to race in the endurance events, which made up the sports car world championship in 1990 and 1991.

According to the Grand Prix Hall of Fame: 'Opportunity arrived when Jordan's Formula One driver Bertrand Gachot found himself in jail and Schumacher was given a test with the Irish team. His times were a revelation and he was quickly signed, or so it was thought. Jordan wanted to sign the young driver to a three-year contract but Schumacher's advisers urged caution. Eventually a temporary deal was done and the rest, as the saying goes, is history.' He made a brilliant debut at Spa in Belgium in a Jordan, where he qualified seventh ahead of his more experienced team-mate. After some legal wrangling that was only recently resolved, he finished the year at Benetton. The next year he won his first race at Spa. Showing signs of brilliance, his time would come in the black year of 1994 when he became world champion. In 1995 after a hard and some-times controversial battle with Damon Hill he became the youngest double champion. 1996 saw him move to Ferrari and marked the start of his biggest challenge.

Three years later at the start of the 1999 season Schumacher had not won the title for four years. Nor had Ferrari for 20. The strain for anyone involved with the Maranello team was unbearable and, as the *Daily Telegraph* reported in March that year, 'Schumacher is the subject of close scrutiny for the signs of a first grey hair. Not through financial worries, of course – he lives with his wife and children in deep comfort in Switzerland, and has a contract worth around £90 million, which runs until 2002. Not bad for the son of a bricklayer.'

So why, at the age of 30, does a husband and father and multi-millionaire find it necessary to continue taking such huge risks?

'Schumacher is worried about something more fundamental – himself,' wrote Timothy Collins. 'The inner ring of confidence that has driven him into glorious limelight and undignified scraps and scrapes has been questioned. He has not won a championship since 1995 and is no longer regarded as an habitual race-winner, unless everything is working perfectly.'

Schumacher can't quit until he is crowned speed king once again. It is a worrying situation for his family because while he continues to pursue fading dreams of further championship glory at terrifying velocity he remains in danger of losing everything. On the eve of the 1999 season he admitted: 'I have responsibilities as a husband and father and sometimes they weigh heavy on my mind. I am under no illusion about the dangers I face every time I go out on to the track. But I am still driven by the same ambition that led me to compete in Formula One in the first place. I can't stop yet.'

A few years earlier Schumacher said this: 'You know, in F1, you can learn in one year what you might take 10 years to learn in another career. It is so intense. You have to cope with the pressure from everyone and the work. It is very hard. It has been hard for me and for my family, but I love it and I work very hard to succeed. My family remains very close with me too. Besides, I love motor racing and I can't imagine life without it. There are many other things I want to do, other ambitions, but there will be plenty of time to do them when my career is over. I am not tempting fate by saying this, I am a survivor and I plan to live to a good old age.'

Ominously, Schumacher's fellow countryman Rudolf Caracciola said the same thing at roughly the same age. The International Motor Sports Hall of Fame tribute says: 'Rudolf "Rudi" Caracciola was considered one of the greatest of Grand Prix drivers, winning more than 225 races during his career of 30 years, and claiming three European Driving Championships, the equivalent of today's Formula One World Drivers' Championship.'

A native of Remagen, Germany, Caracciola discovered a love for automobiles at an early age, and became an apprentice at the Farnir auto works in Dresden. After the First World War, he became a salesman for Farnir, and began racing their cars to promote sales. He fell in love with speed, and tried to gain the attention of the factory-backed teams at Mercedes Benz and elsewhere. He won his first race in 1923 in a four-cylinder car at Berlin Stadium.

Caracciola began driving for Mercedes in some of their less significant races, but in 1926 he got his big break. With the factory team in Spain for an important race, there was no one to enter the initial German Grand Prix. He talked Mercedes into loaning him a car, and went on to win in driving rain. He joined the factory team soon after, winning several races over the next four years; Caracciola was out of a job when the Depression forced Mercedes to suspend their racing operation. He bought his own car with the last of his savings, and won the Irish Grand Prix.

In 1931, he became the first foreigner to win Italy's 1,000-mile Mille Miglia. The next year, he won 10 races for Alfa Romeo, while his team-mate Tazio Nuvolari won six. In 1933, he shattered his thighbone in a crash at the first event of the year at Monaco, and missed the entire year.

In 1935, back with Mercedes, he won his first European title, beating a young Auto Union driver named Bernd Rosemeyer. In the next two years, Caracciola and Rosemeyer swapped European championships, with Rudi prevailing again in 1937. His friendship ended tragically when the two were chasing world speed records in 1938 on the autobahn, and Rosemeyer's car crashed and exploded. Caracciola went on to win his third championship, but something was gone from his driving.

In December 1938, in an interview with a Swiss newspaper, Caracciola said: 'It would make sense to me, my family, and friends if I stopped racing now. But I can't quit yet. I am driven by ambition to become the best. When I'm not racing my life is empty. I will carry on until the desire has gone. I'm not sure when that will be.'

In 1939, Caracciola again won the German Grand Prix but he fled to Switzerland and retired when Hitler tried to 'honour' him with a Nazi title. He did not race again until 1946, when he entered the Indy 500, but he was severely injured in a crash while trying to qualify. After that he raced on a limited basis, and also did high-speed testing for Mercedes. He raced for the last time in a sports car race at Berne, when his career was ended by another crash. He died of cancer in Kassell, Germany, in 1959.

During his prime Caracciola possessed all the attributes that are now hallmarks of the Schumacher phenomenon. In a dossier sent to Hitler, a German newspaper described Caracciola as 'ruthless, dedicated, prepared to go to any lengths to succeed. Lacking emotion, an efficient machine.'

Here are some of the things said about Schumacher sixty years later:

*Michael's ruthless. He's dedicated, he knows what to do and he goes out and does it.*

FORMULA ONE BOSS BERNIE ECCLESTONE

*He's very calm. For five years I worked with Jean Alesi and he was good, but very up and down. Very emotional. Michael is totally different. He lacks emotion. He's like a filter – none of the rubbish gets through. He's totally concentrated.*

RACE ENGINEER IGNAZIO LUNETTA

*He is prepared to go to any lengths to succeed. He is like a machine.*

AYRTON SENNA

The irony here is that Senna was more cold and clinical. He was much more of a machine than Schumacher. Race engineer Pat Symonds said: 'Ayrton was a little too focused on motor racing, I always suspected. Michael is more balanced and rounded. Away from the track, having a meal maybe, listening to him talk about his family or asking about my kids, I sense that if he did a job in a bank or office, and happened to move in next door, he could easily become a mate.

'Both were clearly capable of outclassing most of the rest. But even Senna was not as clever as Schumacher at the same age, not so capable of his grasp of detail. When he started, Michael used to make silly mistakes, over-revving the engine on the first lap. We realized then he only knows one way to drive – flat out. It is not being flash, it is his style; going fast as he can from the start. You could tell Senna was far enough to coast; with Michael, it would be pointless.'

What is not pointless for Schumacher, however, is beating his own limits. It is this obsession with pushing back the boundaries of personal achievement that will keep Schumacher in the danger zone of Formula One until he has had enough of risking his life in pursuit of racing excellence, or becomes a victim of the world's most dangerous sport.

Remember what Senna said about obsession and limits? 'If I am obsessive it is in a positive way. I have a strong natural push but it is not unhealthy, not a disease. I have to establish for myself my own limits. When I have reached those limits I want to beat them and establish new ones. I still don't know how far I can go. I have an understanding of what I am doing, but I don't know how far it will take me.'

Tragically, it took Ayrton Senna into a concrete wall at 193 mph. At the corner of Imola they call Tamburello, Senna's obsession with pushing limits to the extreme dissolved into thin air. He said he had discovered the true meaning of life. In his case it was faith in God. For Jacques Villeneuve it is acceptance of the turning of the wheel of life, for Schumacher it is self-awareness. But it is not enough. Time and time again racing drivers are damaged by the extreme nature of their chosen profession, reach out – or inward – for some peace of mind, only to crave more of the extreme because they can't live without it.

It is not a new thing. Years before their respective lives even began, Bernd Rosemeyer embraced religion after experiencing what he described as 'a feeling of deep anxiety' following a near miss during a race in Germany. Rosemeyer, like Rudolf Caracciola, had a ruthless, machine-like streak but both men were unnerved by near-death experiences. Caracciola used to spend hours in deep meditation. He was not a particularly religious man but his escape from the stress of motor racing was quasi-spiritual. 'Sometimes I have to be alone, with my thoughts and innermost feelings. More and more I need this special time to keep me focused on what is important in life,' he is quoted as saying. 'Sometimes I wonder if it is worth the cost, but in truth I have to carry on. I have to beat my own limits.'

Sound familiar? Rosemeyer also echoed Senna's thoughts before his life ended in the same grotesquely spectacular fashion. While Senna became a born-again Christian, Rosemeyer embraced religion in a less obvious way. He started reading the Bible and kept a prayer book in his travel bag.

But, like Senna, spiritual enlightenment failed to satisfy Rosemeyer's hunger for the thrill of motor racing. In 1938 he said: 'There is something inside me that won't allow me to rest. It keeps pushing me to beat my own achievements.'

The similarity between Rosemeyer's and Senna's philosophy is uncanny. In 1992 Senna said: 'I don't feel happy if I'm comfortable. I have to keep pushing to beat my own achievements.'

In 1939, at the end of the Grand Prix season Rosemeyer, driving for Mercedes, decided to undertake an attempt to regain the land speed record from rival team Auto Union. The attempt would take place on the Frankfurt-Darmstadt-Heidelberg autobahn.

Rosemeyer in describing his record-setting run stated that 'at about 240 mph the joints in the concrete road surface are felt like blows, setting up a corresponding resonance through the car, but this disappears at a greater speed. Passing under bridges the driver receives a terrific blow to the chest, because the car is pushing air aside, which is trapped by the bridge. When you go under a bridge, for a split second the engine noise completely disappears and then returns like a thunderclap when you are through.'

According to the Grand Prix Hall of Fame, on 27 January 1938 Alfred Neubauer checked with the weather bureau at Frankfurt airport and learned that conditions would be ideal the next morning but that the wind would pick up after 9 a.m. At eight Caracciola was off and the record at 268 mph belonged to the three-pointed star. 'I was unnerved,' Caracciola would say. 'The road seemed like a narrow white band, the bridges like tiny black holes ahead. It was a matter of threading the car through them ...'

Rosemeyer was one of the first to congratulate Caracciola and said, 'My turn now.' Caracciola, aware of the prediction for strong winds, sought to warn his young rival but was assured by Rosemeyer that he was one of the 'lucky ones'. Just before noon Rosemeyer entered the closed-cockpit special and rocketed down the autobahn.

Travelling at over 270 mph a crosswind caught his car and caused the Auto Union to somersault, flinging Rosemeyer to his death. Neubauer, Caracciola and von Brauchitsch, his Mercedes rivals, sat silently for a long time, 'unmoving like statues' in Caracciola's words. Record breaking was over for now. 'Bernd literally did not know fear,' Rudolf Caracciola said of his great rival, 'and sometimes that is not good. We actually feared for him in every race. Somehow I never thought a long life was on the cards for him. At first he had no fear, then when he did start to fear the consequences of his love for speed he ignored it. He was bound to get it sooner or later ...'

If fear is the key then maybe Jacques Villeneuve is right. It is better to squeeze the fear than let it squeeze you. It is better to play danger at its own game. Race side by side with death and embrace the unknown.

For these extreme views Jacques Villeneuve has been called an arrogant adrenaline junkie, a space cadet, a shock jock, a suicide case. But as the *Times* journalist Michael Calvin reported in 1997, 'to confront the realities of mortality, it is not that easy to marginalize Jacques Villeneuve'.

He abhors the selective morality that dismisses the death of his friend, Roland Ratzenberger, and deifies Ayrton Senna, who lost his life 24 hours later on a weekend in 1994 that irrevocably altered the shape of his sport. He is prepared to articulate the unthinkable;

to criticize the conventional wisdom that safety requires the emas-
culation of great circuits and encourages mediocrity, in men and
machines. This does not make him popular.

If Formula One is a circus then Villeneuve, and his father before
him, are trapeze artists working without a safety net. And there is an
unspoken law among circus people: when a high-wire star is killed
by a fall, bring on the clowns and make the funeral a celebration of
courage and passion.

That is why Villeneuve sometimes reacts angrily when he is asked
a question about death in motor racing. Tragedy is a recurring
theme but Villeneuve said: 'Why can't we let people rest in peace? It
is the same whenever we race at Imola. People want to bring up the
past. They ask me if I am feeling okay. It is ridiculous.

'Of course I was affected by Imola '94, but that was not just
because of Senna's death. I'm sad to say that if only Roland had died
that weekend, nothing would have been done. As soon as Ayrton
died they felt they had to react, or had to be seen to react. He was a
huge figure, loved by millions and people felt his loss personally.

'Safety is a good thing, but not when it destroys what racing is all
about. Imola is now one of the worst circuits, a disgusting track.
They just put chicanes everywhere. It's safer, but it's not fun to drive.
It's no good for racing.

'There's an awful political correctness about Formula One and
anywhere you find political correctness, it changes the rules.
Everyone keeps a straight face, or smiles and agrees with everything.
I prefer to say what I think. I don't really care if I'm judged arrogant
because of that. I don't force myself to say things to get a reaction. I
say what I truly believe, deep down inside. There are not many
drivers who are listened to, which is a shame because they are the
guys who risk their lives.'

Villeneuve's blue-green eyes may glaze over at the mention of his
late father Gilles, or Roland Ratzenberger or any of the other brave
drivers who died in action. But he does not despise the sport for
killing them or feel sorry that many of the victims of this deadly
obsession die young.

'People want to become racing drivers because, as kids, they see
them as superheroes,' he said. 'You see them pushing their limits as
human beings, overcoming their fears and you are just so impressed.
If Formula One is to be a sport rather than a show, the stakes need to
be high.

'Nobody is looking to kill themselves, that would be pure stupidity, but there needs to be that small sense of danger, that feeling that if you go one kilometre an hour quicker you are going to lose it. That's when it becomes mental. You can feel your body, feel the car getting light. When you are riding on that edge you are in a different world. Nothing else exists at all. All your being is dedicated to that moment. You are striving for perfection, in yourself and your car.'

Michael Calvin wrote: 'There may be a mystical sense of purpose to such sentiments, but they belie Villeneuve's fierce pragmatism.' This is true. Villeneuve's attack on the increasing safety measures designed to slow speeds is measured and based on the experience of countless hours of testing and racing. Villeneuve is many things, but he is not a hypocrite. It is simply that he expects everyone else to perform on that extreme rim of danger and speed. He believes without a shadow of doubt that men who drive racing cars should perform always at the limit and always one mistake away from death.

'All of these safety measures scare me, because it is not going to be Formula One any more,' he said. 'It will destroy racing as it exists. It is a joke. It will not be pure any more. They might as well tell us to buy Formula Three cars and pretend it is Formula One. Everything will be levelled downwards. Anyone will be able to drive because the mechanical and human limits will be so much lower.

'There will be no risk, no rush. There will be no precision in the driving. It will all be numb. You'll lose all control, basically. You'll just be along for the ride. That's a big mistake. At least in the past you have to reach inside yourself to find the strength to do a quick lap. But now the fun is disappearing and the mediocre drivers will be able to hide. They'll be closer to the good guys and the best won't really be needed.

'Formula One must be the ultimate in motor sport and I'm in it to race, not just collect the money. It might be ten times safer than before, but what good is that if we are not doing something special? Danger is not a bad thing; it doesn't have to be negative. Risks are there to be taken. It is good and natural that a man should reach beyond his limits and push back the boundaries of fear. Step into the unknown. We should feel the fear and do it anyway.'

Hold that thought and remember the many Grand Prix drivers killed because of their deadly obsession with power and speed. They believed they were doing something special. And they were: reaching beyond their limits and pushing back the boundaries of fear. Racers until the end.

## 18

# Tales of the Unexpected

*Anything can happen in motor racing, and it usually does.*

MURRAY WALKER

Martin Brundle's philosophy of life is not what you would expect from a man who has cheated death more than once during his motor racing career. 'I don't believe in miracles or fate, and superstition is for those who are not in control of their own lives,' he says. 'I've had a few lucky escapes and people say "Someone up there must like you," or "Hey, perhaps you should quit before your luck runs out," suggesting that an accident is some kind of warning. Rubbish. It's a dangerous sport, accidents happen, and a racing car driver might "cheat death" many times. Fortune favours the brave and this game is all about guts.'

Brundle has plenty of those, but he's a little short on empathy for those who go along with the line of reasoning that says racing car drivers are perhaps more in tune with intangibles than most. As for the theory of premonition and the suggestion that living such an extreme existence puts a man in touch with his spiritual side, Brundle isn't interested. Although there was a brief moment, during the accident that should, by all accounts, have ended his life, when the British Grand Prix driver became detached from his own no-nonsense reality. Then, in the sudden onset of disaster, Brundle thought about God, even though he is a non-believer.

The date was 10 March 1996. The place Albert Park raceway, Melbourne, Australia. Martin Brundle will never, ever forget what happened. It will stay with him for the rest of his life, although time fades even the most vivid memory and listening to Brundle recall the incident now is something of an injustice to the sheer horror of it all. It really was that bad.

This terrifying crash during the first minutes of official race action in the 1996 Formula One world championship projected the most striking image ever seen on television of a driver's brush with death and, strangely, his motivation as well.

In the type of grotesquely dramatic accident that constitutes every driver's nightmare, Brundle became a passenger, flying upside down at 185 mph, as his car disintegrated around him. The Jordan, squeezed in a 180 mph traffic jam at turn three on the first lap of the Australian Grand Prix, was launched into a horrifying barrel-roll before landing upside down and splitting in two on impact.

David Coulthard, whose McLaren slewed across the track, inadvertently forming a launch pad with Johnny Herbert's Sauber, was not the only observer to fear the worst. 'I thought Martin was dead,' Coulthard admitted, though he forced himself to push the prospect out of his mind. Herbert could not forget the freeze-frame image of Brundle soaring 15 feet over his head, completely inverted.

Liz Brundle, watching a television monitor at the back of the garage occupied by the Jordan team, was horribly aware of a sudden silence which spread quickly through the 154,000 crowd in Albert Park. 'I thought, "Oh my God,"' she said. 'Not a lot frightens me, but that took my breath away. I was in shock. It was the worst feeling I've had watching Martin in Formula One.'

She was shaking as the clouds of dust, which had obscured the final stages of her husband's barrel-roll towards a concrete wall, began to clear. Brundle crawled out of the wreckage head first. He had felt fear only once, when he felt something dripping on to his flameproof overalls as he hung by his seatbelts. In fact, it was merely his drink bottle that had leaked, but his mind flashed back to Formula One's last spectacular accident, when Ukyo Katayama's helmet filled with fuel as he somersaulted down the straight at Estoril the previous year during the Portuguese Grand Prix.

Katayama's Tyrrell was sent spiralling when he trapped his front left wheel in between the two right wheels of Luca Badoer's Minardi. His car took off, rolling sideways, before smashing against the trackside barriers. It then rebounded across the asphalt, end on end, before landing upside down. For what must have seemed like an eternity Katayama was trapped in the wreckage while his helmet filled with fuel. One spark and he would have become a human torch, but incredibly he escaped with slight injuries and was detained in hospital for less than 48 hours.

Brundle's escape was even more incredible. 'I just wanted to get the hell out of that car,' he said. 'When I was hanging there, at a bad angle, I thought to myself "You're not going to be able to get out of this".'

It wasn't until the following day that the full impact of his accident sank in. He walked slowly around the remnants of a car that represented an annual investment of £25 million and just shook his head in disbelief. The carbon-fibre survival cell was intact, but the skeletal frame of the engine was contorted, and the rest of the car torn in two at a point just behind the driver's seat by the prolonged violence of the accident.

Brundle exclaimed, with a sense of wonder, 'I've never destroyed a Formula One car like that. Being launched in the air is the accident drivers fear most. You can cope with anything when the car keeps on the road, but when you're flying you're totally out of control.

'If you risk your neck all you ask for in those circumstances is a fair chance to survive. I was sitting there, minding my own business, when the cars in front of me just seemed to trip over each other. I can remember everything from then on in slow motion. The laws of physics meant there was no way I was going to stop. I just went over and over. It was like one of those fairground rides where all the change falls out of your trouser pocket. It seemed to go on for ever and ever.'

Brundle, after a brief conversation with medical staff who had rushed to the scene, jogged the half-mile back to the pit lane. First, he had to convince Professor Sid Watkins, the neurosurgeon who is a key figure in Formula One's safety campaign, of his fitness to drive. Once Brundle had answered his first question correctly – 'What month is it?' – he gave the go-ahead.

'I had no doubts about letting Martin drive,' he explained. 'He had already had a check at the scene. He ran 200 yards to get to me and then ran back to the garage so he was obviously fit.'

Ironically, as it was to turn out, Brundle was suffering from his athletic exertions. He had not jogged on tarmac since smashing both ankles in a crash in Dallas, and was in considerable pain. The grandstand, basking in the warm afternoon sunshine, rose as one as he sprinted back to the Jordan garage. Awe was in the air, and Brundle waved back.

He was greeted by Eddie Jordan, the team owner, who was sweating profusely after running the length of the pit lane. A doctor hovered nearby, insisting: 'If he feels dizzy, or complains of a headache, make sure he comes back in.' Brundle swept past his wife, who had been comforted by Barry Sheene, the former world motor-cycling champion who was commentating on the race for Australian television.

Brundle changed his crash helmet, took two hasty swigs from a bottle of mineral water and pulled on his fireproof face mask. Within a minute, he had squeezed himself into the cockpit of the spare Jordan and accelerated towards the end of the pit lane.

His trials were not over. Mechanics were forced to change three wheels in the four minutes before the restart, which was further complicated by a sudden gearbox problem. Brundle had completed a single lap after the restart when he approached the fateful turn three. Pedro Diniz (Ligier) braked absurdly early, right in front of him. Brundle spun out because his brakes had not warmed up sufficiently, stalled and was packing to leave long before eventual winner Jacques Villeneuve finished.

All that remained was a telephone call to his Norfolk home to reassure his two children that he was all right before they saw the pile-up on television. He said: 'I tell you, this has been the weekend from hell ...'

It was a truly terrifying experience for Brundle, the oldest driver in the field on that day, and he said later that the whole thing seemed to have gone on for a very long time – long enough for him to think about the chances of surviving and say a quick prayer while trying to keep his head down. 'The car just kept rolling over and over,' he said, 'and when I stopped, I could feel fluid coming out. I thought it was petrol but it wasn't, it was coming out of my drink bottle. I was fine. When I got out I was, like, "Oh shit, that's made a mess of that."

'The fact that I was still in one piece hadn't really sunk in, although I could sense that most people could not quite believe that Martin Brundle was still alive. It was a strange feeling.'

Honest, open and direct, Brundle sees that when you ask whether his Melbourne accident affected him in any way, what you probably want to know is did he consider quitting? The answer is he didn't, neither did he suffer from nightmares, panic attacks, anxiety, or any of the other psychological problems wrongly associated with his near-fatal experience.

'It's quite boring really, my reaction to the accident,' he says. 'I'll never forget about what happened, but I didn't give it a second thought after I'd got over the initial shock. There are worse things in life and quite frankly I get tired of all the psychobabble. I had a near miss, got lucky, so what. It's no big deal.'

But that's Brundle all over. He takes most things in his stride and it is a measure of his professionalism that few people are aware that during the weeks and months surrounding the Melbourne accident he suffered the loss of his father and anxieties about his son's health. 'I don't feel like the crash affected me,' he said then.

'I've had a very traumatic time, one way or another, with all sorts of things going on. I've been through probably the most difficult period of my life and that certainly hasn't helped, but I'm a professional sportsman and I can rise above that.'

He adopted the same self-controlled attitude when his friend and long-time rival Ayrton Senna lost his life at Imola. There was a lot of talk within Formula One at the time about the effect of Senna's death on other drivers. The Brazilian was an indomitable figure in Formula One, with an invincible quality.

Of course, other great drivers had perished before him and their tragic demise sent shock waves through the sport. His was the 17th fatality in 30 years of Grand Prix racing, but the most numbing. It chilled Formula One to the bone. It made everyone feel vulnerable. It weakened the gods of speed, the stars of the track, into mere mortals.

For an awful moment, everyone was afraid of the terrible killing force of Formula One. It had ended Senna so brutally, so suddenly. And if it could end Senna, who had an unshakeable faith in God and was the greatest of all Grand Prix drivers, it could certainly end everyone else who dared to tempt fate by risking all in this deadly game of power and speed. As one deeply traumatized Imola track official poignantly remarked in the aftermath of Senna's horrific accident: 'Formula One is thinking now; listen to how quiet the world is. It is searching its soul, reasoning: f— the fame and fortune, f— the money, and f— the glory. It's not worth the cost.'

Brundle did a little soul-searching of his own after his miraculous escape in Melbourne, almost two years after Senna's death, but neither incident was menacing enough to frighten him into quitting. Of course Brundle, like many of the other Formula One drivers, weighed up the risks. It's a natural reaction in the face of such tragedy but the fame and fortune, the money and the glory, outweighed the cost. 'When Senna died, a lot of drivers took a good hard look at the sport,' Brundle said. 'There were a lot of questions asked; questions about the safety of the sport and the sense of the sport, but no one thought about quitting.

'Senna's death was a tragedy but so is every death or serious injury in motor racing. My accident was a reality check but so is every accident in motor racing. These things happen, irrespective of whether a person believes in God or not. It's a dangerous sport. Full stop.'

These days Brundle spends most of his time in Formula One on the safe side of the race track, providing incisive commentary for TV, but he has seen it all before with most other teams on the grid. He shrugged off Senna's death and the death of other drivers in the same composed, ultra-professional manner with which he reacted to his brush with death in Australia.

Three years with Tyrrell as a brave rookie, a desultory season with now-defunct Zakspeed, a one-off outing for Williams as a stand-in, two aimless years with the dying Brabham team, two with Ligier and one apiece with rising Benetton, in 1992, and declining McLaren, in 1994, are littered with near misses and bad smashes. Since his debut in Brazil in March 1984 Brundle has had plenty of reasons to quit, his broken legs in Dallas and grotesquely spectacular crash in Melbourne being two of the most persuasive.

It was only with Benetton, in 1992, that he had an opportunity to realize the promise of 1983 when he had won nine Formula Three races against Senna. But then he came up against the emerging Michael Schumacher and ran out of luck despite claiming five podium finishes and scoring points in 11 of the 16 races. Political intervention meant he was ousted in favour of an Italian driver, Riccardo Patrese, in 1993.

He should have known fortune was reluctant to favour him – in his Formula One debut season, he finished second in only his eighth race for Tyrrell, but had the result and all his points for the season annulled because of a technical infringement by the team. One race later, he broke both ankles.

But his desire to pursue dreams of glory at terrifying speeds always got the better of him until, quite sensibly, with his career in decline, he decided he was getting a little too long in the tooth to continue in what is predominantly a young man's game. Even so, Brundle still has racing fire burning in his veins.

'The motivation never goes,' he said. 'The desire is always there. I can't explain, but maybe it's something you are born with.'

Perhaps Brundle's mother is to blame for her son's obsession with speed and danger. When Martin Brundle would race home from school on his moped and then disappear for hours on end building racing cars, Mrs Brundle was understanding to the point of encouragement; she did autocross and rally driving herself.

After training as a car salesman at the family dealership near King's Lynn in Norfolk, Brundle's self-directed route through racing went via touring cars, a spell in Formula Ford 2000 which nearly broke the family business, and saloon cars with Stirling Moss and Audi. Then he talked BP into sponsoring him in Formula Three, and in his second year 'had a ding-dong with Ayrton Senna for the championship' and was promoted to Formula One.

He was 24 but his battle with the Brazilian helped make him as a racing driver. 'It was worth several years experience,' recalled Brundle, who once left Senna only half a car's width, which he decided to take. The last Brundle saw of Senna was the rivets on the underside of the Brazilian's car in his mirrors. 'He came down to earth, kept his foot in, and tried to T-bone me at the next corner,' Brundle said. 'He missed me and hit a breakdown truck. A very driven man!

'He hated me. I was the first driver to beat him in a straight fight, circuit-racing. And I was the British boy in the British Formula Three championship. We had three big crashes and he had his licence endorsed after one of them and I didn't – and he felt the whole of the administration was against him. In later years, when I saw his outburst when he got run off the road by Alain Prost in Suzuka – well, I'd already seen that from him sitting in stewards' meetings in Formula Three at somewhere like Snetterton.'

But there was evidence of Senna's genius, too. Brundle recalls leading Senna into a long corner at Silverstone in the wet, noticing Senna in his mirror sweeping across to the outside, 'so deep that I thought he had gone off – only for him to reappear in front of me.'

Senna won the battle that year, though it went down to the last race. 'On the podium he was very magnanimous,' Brundle added. 'He went on about me being the best British driver since Jim Clark and what a great driver I was. It was easy for him to be magnanimous, though, because he had won the championship and I had lost it.'

Like Senna, Brundle made a lightning start in Formula One. He was fifth in his first race, second in his seventh. 'I felt invincible. I had a huge accident in Monaco, which I walked away from, just to confirm I was invincible. And then I hit a wall in Dallas and smashed my legs to pieces.'

He recovered to have a respected if largely undynamic career. He raced for eight teams; he managed 10 podium finishes; and he made enough money to buy, among other things, a house in the south of Spain where he spends summers with his wife and two children. But there were no victories. His one full year at the sharp end of the grid – with Benetton, partnering Schumacher – just happened to be the year of the all-conquering 1992 Williams. A sense of incompleteness still haunts him, but like Gerhard Berger, and other drivers, Brundle knows how lucky he is to be able to enjoy life after racing.

Even so, for almost three years he has had a clause in his television contract enabling him to walk if a Grand Prix drive came up. Brundle's love of the thrill of motor racing is a long time dying. The difference between him and his now departed friend and rival Ayrton Senna is a degree of luck. The gods of motor racing smiled on Senna for a long time and often frowned on Brundle. But now people look at Brundle and see a walking, talking miracle – while all that is left of Senna are memories.

## 19

# Die Hard the Brave

*The best risk is the one you control yourself. The one I hate and would never take is the risk you can't control.*

ALAIN PROST

Alain Prost believes in miracles but not motor racing miracles. According to the four-times world champion, miracles, in the true sense of the word, belong in the world outside motor racing. 'There are no extraordinary, supernatural happenings in Grand Prix,' he said, 'only good driving, well-made racing cars, or good fortune. When a driver walks away from a bad crash it is usually because of high safety standards and not God.'

For Prost, a man once dubbed 'the professor' for his detailed analysis of the driver's art, belief in the existence of a power more influential than the combined force of desire and skill and technology is for those who cannot face up to the reality of a sport fundamentally extreme but hedged about with tangibles. Nothing in Formula One is left to chance. 'We [the F1 teams] control the risks,' added Prost, who now runs his own racing team after retiring at the end of the 1993 season. 'My ideal was to go as fast as possible without taking any risks.'

Prost wants his drivers to adopt the same philosophy; the opposite of Ayrton Senna's idea which was to go as fast as possible and take as many risks as necessary to win. 'Yes, he did that,' Prost says of his former enemy. 'Ayrton raced at his limit, the edge of sanity. I would never accept that as the way to race. I did not tread into the unknown. Instead I performed without going to what I thought was my limit. I always say that my ideal was to get pole with the minimum effort, and to win the race at the slowest speed possible.'

Prost's philosophy of well-being and common sense and sanity got under Ayrton Senna's skin. He could not understand anyone not being prepared to race at the limit, or on the edge of acceptable behaviour. The Brazilian went to the edge, or 'The Gates', every time he raced. Towards the end of his career, especially in the 18 months before Imola, Senna went to the edge professing faith in God as some guarantee of invincibility.

Prost once compared Ayrton Senna to an Islamic fanatic – a man prepared to die for his cause. He simply could not believe Senna's commitment or his arrogance and, during their years together at Marlboro McLaren, he made his views clear many times, most notably after near-collisions or crashes which settled races or championships.

Their partnership, such as it was, became one of the most infamous and bitter rivalries not only in Grand Prix racing, but also in the history of sport. They were the two greatest drivers of their era, locked together in the same team, paid by the same masters, yet fighting over every millisecond of potential advantage and every millimetre of track.

In the words of *Daily Telegraph* motor racing journalist Timothy Collings, 'It was a dangerous liaison between a methodical European and a passionate Latin American which reached its nadir at the 1989 Japanese Grand Prix when they collided at the chicane, two great champions brought to a halt in a relationship soured to poison by their scrap over another title.'

Time, however, heals everything and each year when the modern Formula One circus arrives at Imola, Prost is one of the men most deeply saddened that the San Marino Grand Prix will always be a painful reminder of his old rival's death.

It was during that black weekend in May 1994 that Prost and Senna had repaired their relationship to the point where friendship was possible. After so many years of bitter rivalry, they were in the process of making a peace which Senna's family maintained by welcoming the Frenchman among them in Brazil at the funeral and again the following year before the Brazilian Grand Prix. Prost, humbled by his own feelings, now prefers to forget the negative side of his past strife with Senna.

'He is so much missed,' said Prost. 'We have all had to get used to the fact that Ayrton Senna is not among us, but we know too that

Formula One must continue. I think that Ayrton would have understood.

'I learned so much from him and from Brazil, from the Brazilian people, following his death. When he died, I did not feel like going to his funeral in São Paulo. I was concerned that the Brazilian people would feel badly towards me, because of what had happened between us in the past. But I decided to go and the Brazilians rewarded me for coming to the funeral with great sympathy, and from that I learned a great lesson in humility.

'His father and his sister asked me also to take a major part in the launch of the Ayrton Senna Foundation. I was delighted with this because it helps me to give something back to his country and to give something back to him. He was such a big part of my life and my career.'

Prost, who retired a year before Senna's death, said that the Brazilian had asked him several times to return to Grand Prix racing to brighten up the competition. 'His father knew about this,' said Prost. 'He knew how disappointed Ayrton was. When I stopped racing, he approached me more and more to come back and race again. For him, the big thing was the rivalry.'

According to Collings, 'the death of Senna took something extraordinary from Formula One', a fact recognized by Prost. 'We have lost many great names from the sport, like Piquet, Mansell and me, but in normal situations – drivers retiring – and it was simple.

'But for a driver at the top of his career like Ayrton, this was too much. We lost a magic person. Someone who was different from all the others. He had a very different personality. In my opinion, he was a lone star. He was by himself.

'He was special, because of his personality. He gave so much. Generally, I gave 90 per cent to a race, but Senna always gave 100 per cent and expected 105 per cent from the car. He always thought intensely about his racing.'

On the day Senna died, Prost felt very emotional too because Senna talked about him on French television and said he wanted to see Prost race again. 'I thought about this a lot,' Prost admitted. 'It was all a pity because we could have been such friends – our fighting was over then.

'No one in Formula One ever impressed me the way Ayrton did. Only Nelson Piquet and Niki Lauda stand with him for me. But neither of them had the same impact on my career.'

Unlike Senna, Prost the Grand Prix driver did not always look like a winner. His driving style was deceptive and although his determination was clear to see he won many of his races by intelligent strategy rather than dominating speed. In this respect Senna and Prost were very much alike. It was just that Senna raced at the limit and Prost did not. There have been faster drivers than Prost, there have been more audacious drivers, but there have not been any more successful than the Frenchman. At the end of the 1993 season, Prost retired, leaving behind a memorable record of achievements. In his last season he won seven Grands Prix, claimed 13 pole positions, set six fastest laps and was crowned world champion for the fourth time in 13 seasons of Grand Prix racing.

The two main reasons why he won a record 51 Grands Prix are because he had competitive cars and also because he was always motivated to do his job. He was never down, even when people were getting killed or he was in danger of losing his own life.

The great thing about Prost was the way he read a race. From beginning to end he knew how he was going to race and, more importantly, what the other drivers were likely to do – with the exception of Senna who was generally unpredictable and could not be trusted to race by the book.

'It's a natural instinct,' Prost told *Motorsport* in 1997. 'It's the way I worked from the very beginning of my racing career. In Formula Renault everyone had the same tyres, same chassis and same engine. I thought, "Where are you going to do it?" You can't think you are going to win all the races by being quicker, because it's not possible. So you need to find another way. What I did from the first year was to test very often, if the budget allowed, and I would change everything on the car all the time – anti-roll bar, springs, everything; just to understand what was happening on the car.

'I worked very hard and I played around a lot with the weight. We would prepare the cars maybe 10 or 15kg lighter than the limit, because then I could have the rest of the weight as ballast and put it where I wanted. I was very interested in that. It is very important to have confidence as well as to build up experience. I always wanted to feel that I had enough knowledge and experience of the car that I could change its set-up on the grid and still win the race. That is an important part of my success.'

Another big part of Prost's success is that he hated not to finish a race. 'I would prefer to finish sixth rather than lead and then crash or

retire,' he added, 'I have always wanted to finish to get the experience.'

Maybe that was the decisive difference between Prost and Senna
and the reason why the Frenchman is still alive. Senna was always
prepared to risk smashing his car in the pursuit of the quickest lap.

Prost admitted: 'Sometimes I think I could have got some better
results if I had a different mentality; if I could have pushed hard and
attacked. But then I would have had a good chance of making a
mistake. I always thought it was better to be safe and finish third or
fourth than to risk a lot and win or come second. I have always had
this mentality because I hated to break anything on the car.'

One of Prost's best performances was Brazil in 1987, with a
McLaren-Porsche. He was seventh on the grid, about two seconds
behind Nigel Mansell's Williams-Honda. From the beginning of
the Friday before the race Prost worked with McLaren engineer
John Barnard and, without caring about qualifying, they worked on
the best race set-up they could possibly find.

'Everybody was going for high downforce,' Prost recalled.
'Because there was a problem with the tyre wear. We went in the
opposite direction and ran very little downforce. So I would have
to force myself to go slowly through the corners, and we planned to
stop only once. Everybody else was going to stop at least twice, if not
more. I remember in the first part of the race I was sixth and I could
have gone quicker, but I had to go slow. It was one of the most difficult things I have ever done. I stopped only once and I won the race
by 30 seconds, but I'd been two seconds behind in qualifying! When
you win a race like this the feeling is very, very good.

'There have been times when I have been flat out to finish sixth,
but you can't see that from the outside. In 1980 I finished three or
four times in seventh place. I pushed like mad, yet everyone was
gathered around the winner and they were thinking that I was just
trundling around.'

According to Prost, 'The best risk is the one you control yourself.' The one he hated and never took is the risk you can't control.
The sad irony of Senna's fate is that he was a control freak who
sought control of the unknown. Prost knew his limits.

He said: 'I would never, ever go bungee jumping. Why? Because I
have no control. That is what I hate. It's like when people talk about
driving F1 cars in the rain. I have absolutely no problem with it.
People don't understand that it was maybe my biggest pleasure to

drive an F1 car when it's wet. But in conditions like when there was a lot of water and no visibility, it was like Russian roulette. You were not in control.

'You had no visibility: maybe there was a car in front of you, maybe not. At one stage the car in front was 400 metres away and I couldn't see anything. People will mumble and say 'Prost is not brave'. I'm brave. I'm brave to say that I won't take this sort of risk. The people who criticize you will not be the ones taking care of your legs when you are in your wheelchair. People who never drove a car in these conditions, they just don't know.'

Senna could be cold and intense, often complicated to the point of self-denial. Prost is a very warm and uncomplicated man who doesn't rely on passion or inspiration. Neither he nor Senna indulged in showmanship or bravado and they were capable of a level of mental discipline beyond the comprehension of most people. Senna simply ran out of luck. Or possibly he did not have Prost's sense of mortality.

# 20

# Prayer

*Everyone prays to God sometimes, even if you don't believe. It's human nature, especially if you're afraid.*

MIKA HAKKINEN

1998 and 1999 Formula One world champion Mika Hakkinen asked God to spare his life following his near death in Australia in 1995. Afterwards, when he was no longer in danger, the Finnish driver thanked God just in case it was He who pulled him through. Hakkinen was not sure, but anyway the sentiment faded quicker than smoke from a hot exhaust. Five years and a full measure of good fortune and success later, and the 'Flying Finn' barely recalls the desperate request for divine intervention. But at least he is honest about it.

Hakkinen is not a religious man, not even in the vaguest sense of the word. His idea of spiritual enlightenment is closing his eyes while listening to Duran Duran or, at the extreme, looking at cathedral architecture, but he did 'call on God' during the worst moment of his career. 'I said a silent prayer because I was afraid,' he admits, with a sense of awe and reverence that belies the cool, analytical look in his steel-blue eyes. 'In this kind of desperate situation when you are unable to help or protect yourself, when your physical strength is gone and you are emotionally and mentally fighting for your right to live, a person can turn to God. Even if they don't believe. It is a natural reaction.'

The immensely gifted Formula One star, like so many of his contemporaries, is a self-confessed agnostic, if such a thing exists. Hakkinen believes in the strength of the human spirit, the power of the human mind to absorb knowledge and operate effectively and crucially close to the point of emotional, mental and physical tolerance and desire. God may have listened to and answered Hakkinen's prayer on the day when Formula One almost killed its brightest prospect, but raw animal desire – the most base survival instinct and will to win – transformed the McLaren-Mercedes driver from a badly smashed-up piece of human debris to champion of the world in less than three years. That is a miracle in itself because no one, apart from Hakkinen himself, believed it possible.

His near-death experience happened in Adelaide in 1995, during the opening qualifying for the Australian Grand Prix. Hakkinen fractured his skull from ear to ear in a 150 mph crash on Friday 10 November. Those who witnessed the accident thought Hakkinen's life would expire by Saturday. Certainly no one expected him to be alive by the start of Sunday's race, especially after the sickening scenes on the blood- and oil-soaked track where doctors had to perform a tracheotomy because Hakkinen had stopped breathing.

Hakkinen lost control of his McLaren on entry to the high-speed Brewery Corner then hit a kerb, launching into the air before slamming into the barriers. The corner, a fast right-hander between the Jones and Brabham straights, is the quickest on the track and Hakkinen was travelling at about 110 mph when he smashed into the barriers, which are protected by only one wall of tyres.

In his book *Life at the Limit*, Professor Sid Watkins recalled: 'When I arrived at the accident two minutes after the crash he was unconscious and having serious difficulty breathing. We removed him from the car and had to perform a tracheotomy at the trackside. Fortunately, although he had a fractured skull, his brain injury was not severe.'

Hakkinen was in a coma for several days after the accident and was temporarily deaf and blind upon regaining consciousness. Watkins added: 'When I told him that he had had a big accident, his first words were: "Was it my fault?" Reassuring him that it was due to a puncture I gave him further good news that Mr Dennis [McLaren team boss Ron Dennis] was giving him a few days off and that he didn't have to drive in the race the next day.

'He grinned crookedly in response to this and, knowing his sense of humour was recovering, I felt very optimistic about his recovery.'

After several weeks in the Royal Adelaide Hospital, Hakkinen travelled to London for further tests and, five weeks after his injury, he went off to Monaco to convalesce and to start to prepare himself for the 1996 season. Ironically, the experience intensified Hakkinen's desire to become world champion but did little to strengthen what little faith he has in God. Of course, he is thankful for getting another shot at life, and he will never forget the afternoon of Friday 10 November 1995, but he has not prayed since.

'It was a big shock,' he said. 'It took a long time to recover and I had to stay in the hospital for a month or two and then I had to stay home. It was a long process to recover. The doctors didn't allow me to start training again until very late. It was very difficult, emotionally, mentally and physically. I did a lot of thinking after my accident. About everything. I was not scared, but I was different the next time I got in a car. It took me a long time to recover.

'But now I'm sitting here and I'm healthy and I'm a happy chap after winning the championship and everything's fine. That's the way it goes. Of course, the accident I had is there in the back of my mind but that doesn't mean I think about it. When you are here at a Grand Prix there are too many other things to think about.

'Obviously it has changed me but not as much as people think. I think I am more calculated in the way I'm working. Mentally I feel much stronger. That is one of the things that's changed. I feel more relaxed in myself, and I feel I know how to go about my job. I look at things differently when I am driving round the track. It doesn't mean I'm looking at the kerbs and walls and worrying about an accident but I am studying things more carefully.

'I work my way up to the limit slowly now, and I look at high-speed corners and I do sometimes think about the possibility of hurting myself. But that makes me concentrate even more on driving my car as fast and as well as I can and staying on the track. It's a big job but it's always a big job for everybody. I'm just working more at it – which is what I mean about feeling I am mentally stronger than I was before.'

As much as he keeps his distance from religion or quasi-spiritual matters, Hakkinen is, as Ayrton Senna once remarked, a 'soulful' character. Hakkinen is dry-humoured and warm. He is a shy, private man, not afraid to keep himself to himself in a sport awash with showmanship. He is at his most content relaxing with his wife Erja at their Monaco home or visiting mother in Helsinki.

Away from the crowds, when Hakkinen talks, he reveals depths of thought and feeling uncommon in his sport. Only now, after winning the championship with McLaren-Mercedes Benz, is his confidence rising to the levels of earlier days before the death of his team-mate Ayrton Senna and his own life-threatening crash in 1995.

'After that accident, when I recovered,' he said, 'I wasn't exactly hiding, but I was not putting myself in the public view. I was still quite a closed person – maybe I still am – and I didn't let anyone get too near to me. I wasn't strong enough to cope with everything.'

It is a habit he found difficult to break until the European Grand Prix at Jerez in October 1997 when, after 96 attempts, he claimed his maiden victory with an assist from team-mate David Coulthard. The smiles that characterized his face from the first days at Phoenix, where he made his debut for Lotus in 1991, began to return.

'I have been through a lot of experiences,' he said, referring in particular to Adelaide. 'When you go through a situation like that, where you have fought for your life, it does change you a bit.'

Once seen as touched by arrogance and criticized – unfairly and wrongly – for revelling in his third-place finish at the San Marino Grand Prix of 1994, while Senna lay dying (something Hakkinen and the other drivers were not aware of), the Finn is now regarded as modest and sensitive.

'It has been a tough road to get to where I am today,' he added. 'Less fortunate men have failed or died trying. I love motor racing but not as much as I love life. I realized this in those horrific moments immediately after my accident.'

Hakkinen was labelled as the nearly man of Formula One long before he nearly died trying to shake off the unwanted tag. Not that anyone ever really doubted his blistering speed, but somehow Hakkinen had failed to meet his own and his fans' expectations in the sport – until 1998. A near-perfect season with the dominant McLaren team saw Hakkinen clinch his first world championship, just one year after securing his first Formula One race win.

Hakkinen began his racing career in karting, winning the Finnish championship five times between 1974 and 1986. In 1987 he moved up to Formula Ford, winning the Swedish championship. A leap to the Opel Lotus Euroseries in 1988 saw Hakkinen as champion as well as claiming the runner-up spot in the British series.

In 1989 he entered the ultra-competitive world of Formula Three. He finished in seventh overall. The following year saw Hakkinen perform brilliantly to claim the title with West Surrey Racing in a close battle with fellow countryman Mika Salo.

Hakkinen made his debut in Formula One with the Lotus Judd team in 1991, taking the unusual (at the time) step of skipping Formula 3000 altogether. Hakkinen looked completely out of his depth on his debut with the team at Phoenix, Arizona, suffering from a number of spins before finally retiring with engine failure. However, he quickly got used to the demands of Formula One and scored a good fifth place at the San Marino Grand Prix – his third ever Formula One race. Those two points were the only tangible reward of the season and Hakkinen slumped to 15th in the drivers' championship.

Remaining with Lotus in 1992, Hakkinen managed to score 11 points to finish in eighth position in the championship. By this stage it was clear to him that the once-great Lotus team was in dire financial difficulties and it was time to make some decisions.

In a brave move Hakkinen signed up with McLaren – as test driver. The big chance came at the expense of regular McLaren driver Michael Andretti, who had mutually decided to leave Formula One, heading back to the familiar CART environment. Hakkinen was therefore promoted to the race team alongside Ayrton Senna. His debut for McLaren was sensational in that he outqualified Senna. Not many drivers can say that they have ever done that. In the race Hakkinen was running well inside the points before losing control of the McLaren on the final corner and hitting the barriers hard. The next race saw his first ever podium with a fine third position at Suzuka. Hakkinen had done enough to become a regular full-time McLaren driver.

The 1994 season saw the Finnish driver on the podium six times. The Peugeot-powered McLaren was, however, appallingly unreliable, thus blunting any chance for the world championship. On the negative side, Hakkinen had a reputation for mistakes. In typical fashion, he qualified in a brilliant second position at Monaco. At the lights, he completely threw away all his hard work in an unnecessary collision with Damon Hill's Williams at the first corner.

For 1995 McLaren shed their unwanted Peugeot engine and signed a contract with Mercedes. Hakkinen had a good season with fewer mistakes, but only managed to achieve seventh position in the drivers' championship with 17 points, gaining second-place finishes in Italy and Japan. The horrific accident at the season's end in Adelaide left Hakkinen fighting for his life but a winter of recuperation amazingly saw him back in action for McLaren once again in 1996.

Hakkinen only reached the podium on four occasions in 1996, but still managed to finish in fifth position overall. The 1997 season witnessed a somewhat inconsistent performance. The first half of the year saw him well and truly beaten by team-mate David Coulthard. Hakkinen did, however, almost win the elusive first Grand Prix at Silverstone, only for engine failure to deprive him. This sniff of victory seemed to remotivate the popular Finn, as he became the dominant McLaren driver during the latter part of the year. Victory finally came at the end of the year at the European Grand Prix. The victory, while still a victory, was given to the Finn first by team-mate David Coulthard and then by Williams-Renault driver Jacques Villeneuve. It is not the ideal way to win your first race. He deserved better.

And better it got. Making the best of the superb Adrian Newey-designed chassis, Mika Hakkinen drove with precision and determination to record eight victories and take the world championship. Along with the wins came a new-found maturity in his driving – mistakes were rare and the end result was impressive. With a new contract in his pocket with McLaren in 1999 – again alongside Coulthard – Hakkinen has demonstrated speed and for the first time, superb consistency.

So what motivates a man like Mika Hakkinen? He is one of the highest-paid sportsmen in the world with reported earnings of around £15 million a year. Money should be a huge motivating factor for a racing driver simply because he is putting his life on the line every time he does his job. But not for Hakkinen.

He claims: 'To be really honest, I am here to race and to win the races and that's the target and nothing else. The money is naturally more or less the tool that helps you to be a better racing driver. It's the tool to help you progress and it's important, it makes you go faster.'

The pressure, however, remains for a world-class driver to turn in top-notch results, but Hakkinen doesn't let it bother him. Handling pressure, he says, 'is easy when you're young. Your life is not necessarily easier, but the pressure is a different story. When you get older you start understanding more and more and the responsibility goes higher and then the pressure arrives. But you pressure yourself anyway, I think. You yourself are creating the pressure, so you have to learn how to handle it and organize it so you don't put the pressure on yourself.

'If you start thinking [about crashing] it doesn't work. If you start thinking about dying it's not going to work.

'When you're driving you can't start thinking about your girl-friend, or what you'll have for dinner tonight. You're thinking about your racing, your driving, your lines and that's it. If you start thinking about dying you cannot race. That means you have to switch it off, and its not easy but you have to do it.'

As for how the crash affected his driving, Hakkinen, with a smile, explained: 'When I was younger I was taking risks every lap. Now I take risks every second lap.'

# 21

# Another Dimension

*As for the accidents and tragedies – the circus goes on. There is no room for tears.*

FRANÇOIS CEVERT, LESS THAN 24 HOURS BEFORE HE WAS KILLED
DURING PRACTICE FOR THE 1973 US GRAND PRIX

'I never want my children to become too fond of me,' Alberto Ascari confided to a close friend, having narrowly escaped being drowned when his Lancia plunged over the harbour wall at Monte Carlo on the 81st lap of the 1955 Monaco Grand Prix. 'Because one of these days, I may not come back and they will suffer less if I keep them at arm's length.' Four days later, the Italian double world champion was killed test-driving a Ferrari at Monza, leaving a widow and two young children. For some unknown reason Ascari wasn't wearing his helmet.

Ascari believed in fate and God. He said a silent prayer for safety and crossed himself before each race, but he knew there was a good chance motor racing would kill him. Mika Hakkinen doubts whether he could continue to compete in the world's most dangerous sport if he had children. Echoing Ascari's words, Hakkinen admitted: 'Because I know there is a chance that one day I may not come back from a race, I am not sure if I could be a father and still risk my life racing Formula One cars.'

For Damon Hill the prospect of inflicting on his loved ones the agony of permanent hurt and loss became too much to bear. He could not possibly keep his family at arm's length, so he embraced them and let go of motor racing. The bottom line for Hill, Ascari, Hakkinen and many other Grand Prix drivers is this: fatal accidents happen irrespective of children or personal beliefs. How can you promise your family you will always come back from a race, or believe prayers of safety will be answered when you willingly put your life on the line in pursuit of fame and fortune?

Ayrton Senna entertained no such fears, believing himself to be immortal behind the wheel of a Formula One racing car. And on the fifth anniversary of Senna's death, May 1999, Hakkinen, Schumacher, Hill and the rest of the present-day pilots raced around Imola's Tamburello curve without a second's pause. In the words of Frenchman François Cevert, 'As for the accidents and tragedies – the circus goes on. There is no room for tears.' Less than 24 hours after he uttered those words, Cevert, 29, was dead, killed during practice for the 1973 US Grand Prix at Watkins Glen.

Cevert was right, there is no room for tears, not even for the defeated. Tears do not win races; tears do not keep you alive. They are for the dead only. Tears are for mourners, and there are rarely tears of joy. 'There are no tears in heaven,' Senna once said, 'so don't cry for me now or when I'm gone. I plan to live a long, happy life but when the end comes and I go to be with Jesus, I want people to remember me and be happy.'

People certainly remember Senna, but it is not the way he wanted it. He died young and his memory is stained with tears. His grave attracts more visitors than those of John F. Kennedy, Marilyn Monroe and Elvis Presley combined. Even now, all these years later, people still ask why Senna, the greatest driver of his generation, perished on Imola's relatively straightforward if high-speed Tamburello curve. Even an Italian court could not come up with the definitive reason why his Williams-Renault deviated from the normal race line and fatally continued straight on at 192 mph. Mechanical failure ... driver error ... debris on the track ... sudden blackout ... every conceivable – and inconceivable – theory has been voiced.

When Jim Clark, arguably the greatest world champion, was killed at Hockenheim in 1968, New Zealander Chris Amon spoke for every driver before or since when he said: 'As well as the grief, there's another dimension. If it could happen to Jim Clark, what chance do the rest of us have?' A better chance now than ever before, it has to be said, for in the five years since Senna died, safety standards have been improved immeasurably, so much so that the sport that killed him has virtually disappeared, to be replaced with a sterile technological battle.

Senna's crash at Imola triggered a wide-ranging series of reforms to make Formula One safer, including a wholesale redesign of cars. Drivers and team owners all praise the safety principles dictated by Max Mosley, the President of the FIA, Formula One's ruling body, but the realization has dawned that eliminating risk has also eliminated the very element that makes motor racing a sport. Mosley has tried to slow down Formula One by introducing narrow cars with slim, grooved tyres. His logic is difficult to argue against: no matter how powerful the engine, he says, if the car is on bicycle tyres it cannot go quickly. Speed kills, but removing the big risks is killing Formula One. Maybe Jacques Villeneuve is right, the sport is no sport without real danger.

'In these sterile conditions excitement is minimal,' Villeneuve said. 'Races are like a procession because if a driver does not take the lead from the start, he will be unlikely to be able to overtake his way to victory. Formula One is often described as a circus, but a circus is a show and, at the moment, we don't have a show. The way things are at the moment, I am more at risk driving down the street. No one wants to see drivers getting killed or badly hurt, but you can take safety to the extreme. Danger is the big attraction.'

Ironically, while Ascari, Clark, Senna and Jochen Rindt – killed in practice at Monza in 1970 – died in pursuit of speed on the track, three other former world champions lost their lives in equally violent circumstances after retiring: Graham Hill was the victim of a plane crash, Mike Hawthorn's Jaguar was in collision with a lorry on the Guildford bypass, and Giuseppe Farina's Lotus-Cortina skidded into a telegraph pole in the French Alps.

Even the very best, however, accept death as a part of their chosen way of life. 'Not so long ago,' says Jackie Stewart, 'I lay awake in bed and counted all the people I've known who died racing. After a while – maybe an hour – I stopped counting at 57. And I'd only got up to 1972 ...'

Motor racing may be less dangerous now than ever before, but this consuming passion for power and speed will always possess the potential to be lethal. 'It is a deadly obsession,' François Cevert said, a year before he died. 'One mistake, one bit of bad luck, and you're history. But man was born with a spirit of adventure and an appetite for danger. God gave man the instinct to compete and to survive. He also gave us free will. Some men die climbing mountains, other men die racing cars. We all die in the end anyway. Better, though, to burn out than fade away. Better to die for something you believe in than for nothing at all.'

It was Cevert, a formidable number two to Jackie Stewart from 1970 to 1973, who first suggested that Grand Prix racing may be the only sport devoid of atheism. 'Every single driver I have ever known believes in God in some form or another,' he said six months before his death. 'This existence puts you in touch with your spiritual side. Most people think we are a bunch of playboys who don't give a shit about anything except fame and fortune. They are not far from the truth. But behind the playboy exterior, in most cases, are men who have faith in personal beliefs.'

Cevert may be right. When asked if they believed in the existence of God, all the 22 drivers who started the San Marino Grand Prix on 2 May 1999 said yes. It may not mean much in the overall scheme of things but, as Mario Andretti poignantly put it, 'Only a fool would risk his life for a living and not have some faith in God.'

# FIA Formula One World Championship

*Safety in Grand Prix racing in the 35 years from 1963-1998*
*A Study by the Circuits and Safety Department*

This document indicates the development of Formula One racing and the corresponding increase in the number of race incidents, over the period 1963-98, in which unprecedented advances in the application of technology and aerodynamics to the cars produced remarkable potential for increasing performance. It shows for each period considered the continuous action taken by the FIA and the Formula One teams in developing and applying measures to progressively contain the consequences of accidents, latterly achieving levels of risk which are minimal for participants and negligible for spectators.

Although the example of Formula One only is considered here, the increases in both racing activity and safety have been reflected in every branch of motor sport under the control of the FIA.

## PERIOD: 1963–1967

GP races: 50 – Estimated racing kms*: 256,000 – Accidents in races: 47 – Serious injuries, drivers: 2 – Fatalities, drivers: 3 – Fatalities, officials: 0 – Fatalities, spectators: 0

INTRODUCTION OF SAFETY REGULATIONS BY THE FIA

| CARS | CIRCUITS | DRIVERS | ORGANIZATION |
|------|----------|---------|--------------|
| **1963–65**: Pump fuel only. Automatic starter; rollbar; double braking system; rules for seatbelt anchorages, fire protection, fuel tanks, fillers and breathers. | FIA begins to organize circuit safety inspections (previously done by national authorities). | Protective helmet and over-alls obligatory. | **1963**: Flag signalling code. |

*NOTE: 'Estimated racing kms' refers to racing only: practice sessions at evens would increase this by up to 50%.

## PERIOD: 1968–1972

GP races: 59 – Estimated racing kms*: 227,000 – Accidents in races: 88 – Serious injuries, drivers: 3 – Fatalities, drivers: 4 – Fatalities, officials: 0 – Fatalities, spectators: 0.

INTRODUCTION OF SAFETY REGULATIONS BY THE FIA

| CARS | CIRCUITS | DRIVERS | ORGANIZATION |
|---|---|---|---|
| **1963:** Electrical circuit breaker; reverse gear; cockpit designed for easy evacuation; oil catch tank; rollbar 5cm above driver's helmet. | **1970:** Considerations on circuit design published: track verges minimum 3m; double guard rails; spectators at least 3m behind fencing; barrier between pit lane and track; track width, surface and gradient change regulations; straw bales banned; mandatory FIA inspections. | **1968:** Recommendations on seat harnesses, fire-resistant clothing, shatterproof visors. | **1971:** Personnel, equipment and duties specified in race supervision, marshalling, signals. |
| **1969:** Two extinguisher systems; parts with aerodynamic influence must be immobile, fixed to sprung parts of car only; maximum bodywork height and width limits. | **1972:** Circuit Safety Criteria published; debris fence specifications. | **1971:** Max. 5 seconds for driver evacuation from cockpit. | |
| **1970:** Safety bladder fuel tanks. | | **1972:** Six-point harness. Drivers' Code of Conduct published. | |
| | | **1973:** International medical card and examination for all drivers. | |

**1972:** Safety foam in fuel tanks; no magnesium sheet less than 3mm thick; 15W red rear light; headrest; minimum cockpit dimensions; combined electrical cut-off/extinguisher external handle; FIA/spec/FT3 fuel tank.

## PERIOD: 1973–1977

GP races: 77 – Estimated racing kms*: 446,000 – Accidents in races: 250 – Serious injuries, drivers: 5 – Fatalities, drivers: 5 – Fatalities, officials: 1 – Fatalities, spectators: 6 (nb the spectators killed had all penetrated prohibited areas)

### INTRODUCTION OF SAFETY REGULATIONS BY THE FIA

| CARS | CIRCUITS | DRIVERS | ORGANIZATION |
|---|---|---|---|
| **1973:** Crushable structure round fuel tank; no chrome plating of suspension parts. | **1973:** Catch fences; rescue equipment; starting grid dimensions. | **1975:** FIA standard for fire-resistant clothing. | **1973:** Fire service regulations. |
| **1974:** Self-seal breakaway fuel coupling. | **1974:** Catch fences with sand. | **1977:** Helmets must be to FIA-approved standards. | **1975:** Medical service; resuscitation centre; obligatory rescue exercise. |
| **1976:** 'Safety structures' around dashboard and pedals. | **1975:** Marshal posts; service roads. | | **1974:** 2x2 staggered starting grid with 12m length per car. |
| **1977:** Pedalbox protection defined. | **1977:** Gravel arrester beds defined. | | |

## PERIOD: 1978–1982

GP races: 76 – Estimated racing kms*: 399,000 – Accidents in races: 283 – Serious injuries, drivers: 3 – Fatalities, drivers: 3 – Fatalities, officials: 1 – Fatalities, spectators: 0

INTRODUCTION OF SAFETY REGULATIONS BY THE FIA

| CARS | CIRCUITS | DRIVERS | ORGANIZATION |
|---|---|---|---|
| **1978**: Bulkhead behind driver and front rollbar defined. | **1980**: Obligatory permanent medical centre. | **1978**: Licence qualification requirements. | **1978**: Grid 14m per car. |
| **1979**: Bigger cockpit opening; two mirrors; improved extinguisher system. | **1981**: Tyre barriers; pit lane minimum width 10m. | **1979**: Life support system (medical air) obligatory. | **1979**: FIA-appointed permanent race starter. |
| **1981**: Reinforced 'survival cell' introduced and extended in front of driver's feet. | | | **1980**: FIA approval of medical service obligatory; fast rescue car regulations. |
| | | | **1981**: Grid 1x1x1. |

## PERIOD: 1983–1987

GP races: 79 – Estimated racing kms*: 428,000 – Accidents in races: 218 – Serious injuries, drivers: 2 – Fatalities, drivers: 0 – Fatalities, officials: 0 – Fatalities, spectators: 0

INTRODUCTION OF SAFETY REGULATIONS BY THE FIA

| CARS | CIRCUITS | DRIVERS | ORGANIZATION |
|---|---|---|---|
| **1983**: Flat bottom obligatory; skirts banned; red light increased to 21W.<br><br>**1984**: Refuelling in races banned; fuel tank in centre of car.<br><br>**1985**: Frontal crash test. | **1984**: Concrete wall may replace guard rails.<br><br>**1985**: Catch fences banned.<br><br>**1987**: Criteria for temporary circuits. | **1984**: F1 'Super licence' required. | **1986**: Permanent FIA medical service inspector; medical helicopter obligatory.<br><br>**1987**: Grid 16m per car. |

## PERIOD: 1988–1992

GP races: 80 – Estimated racing kms*: 478,000 – Accidents in races: 305 – Serious injuries, drivers: 1 Fatalities, drivers: 0 – Fatalities, officials: 0 – Fatalities, spectators: 0

INTRODUCTION OF SAFETY REGULATIONS BY THE FIA

| CARS | CIRCUITS | DRIVERS | ORGANIZATION |
|------|----------|---------|--------------|
| **1988**: Driver's feet behind front wheel axis; static crash test of survival cell and fuel tank. **1990**: Larger mirrors; quickly detachable steering wheel. **1991**: FIA-tested seatbelts; FT5 fuel tanks; rollbar test; dynamic test of survival cell. **1992**: More serious impact tests: water-filled fuel tank fitted to test strength of seat back bulkhead and 75kg dummy fitted with maximum deceleration figure for the torso (also verifies harness anchorage strength). | **1989**: Trackside barrier min. height 1m; pit wall min. 1m 35. **1992**: Kerbs lowered; pit lane min. width 12m; pit entry chicane obligatory. | **1989**: Dope testing on IOC model introduced. | **1988**: Permanent FIA race director. **1990**: Driver extrication exercise obligatory. **1992**: Safety car introduced. |

## PERIOD: 1993–1998

GP races: 82 – Estimated racing kms*: 450,000 – Accidents in races: 382 – Serious injuries, drivers: 11 – Fatalities, drivers: 2 – Fatalities, officials: 0 – Fatalities, spectators: 0.

### INTRODUCTION OF SAFETY REGULATIONS BY THE FIA

| CARS | CIRCUITS | DRIVERS | ORGANIZATION |
|---|---|---|---|
| **1993**: Headrest area increased (from 80cm$^2$ to 400cm$^2$); front overhang reduced (100cm to 90cm); rear wing height above ground reduced (100cm to 95cm); distance of front wing endplates above the flat bottom increased (25mm to 40mm); complete wheel width reduced (18 to 15in); fuel regulations restricted to permit only fuels of a kind used by the general public. | **1994**: Pits spectator gallery fire shield obligatory; identification of 27 'very high risk' corners by computer analysis: 15 removed from list by 1994 performance reductions; tyre wall deceleration tests, analysed relative to human tolerance levels, produce a standard by which to judge new barriers; use of conveyor belting in front of tyre walls recommended.<br><br>**1995**: Smooth raised kerbs recommended for F1; gravel | **1994**: Approved helmet standards reduced to three most stringent (Sell/BSI/SFI); earphones banned; weight 1800g max.; check-tests made on clothing and helmets in use.<br><br>**1995**: Three-inch wide seat harness shoulder straps obligatory; F1 drivers' Super Licence criteria more stringent.<br><br>**1996**: Safety belt release lever must point downwards. | **1994**: Pit lane speed limited to 80kph in practice, 120kph in the race; fire-protective clothing for all refuelling crews; burns treatment material in each pit obligatory; pit lane access new restrictions; creation of the Advisory Expert Group, to apply new technology to safety in F1.<br><br>**1995**: Minimum safety services recommended for private testing; clarification of blue, yellow and white flags |

1994: Wheels must be made from an homogeneous metallic material; more stringent fire extinguisher regulations; minimum thickness of the headrest 75mm (no minimum previously); cockpit area side load test increased (from 2000daN to 3000daN); driver aids (traction control, antilock and power brakes, automatic gears) banned; four-wheel steering no longer permitted; downforce reduced: smaller front wing endplates, shorter diffuser, deflector panels restricted; pump fuel compulsory; 10mm skid block under reference plane.

1995: Engine capacity reduced: 3.5 to 3.0 litres; chassis must extend at least

bed waves and furrows deleted; first pit wall debris shields installed.

1996: Corners classified 'high risk' reduced to two through circuit safety improvements and track modifications; temporary circuit wall and debris fence specification guidelines; FIA test requirement for 'thin' energy absorbing barriers.

1997: FIA circuit approval required for F1 testing; kerb types and heights standardized after year of investigation; bolted tyre wall construction obligatory; analysis of the performance of safety measures with data recorded on the cars' ADRs.

1997: FIA supervision of conditions for private testing.

1998: Two shoulder strap anchorages recommended; driver must be able to exit and replace steering wheel in 10 seconds.

rules; FIA doctor given tech. assistant.

1996: Standardization of FIA medical and safety cars; improved safety car procedure. Fire exercises with teams; transformation of starting lights and procedure; new 'F1 Safety Commission' including three drivers.

1997: FIA approval for all Chief Medical Officers and medical centres; revised accident intervention plan; safety car: more powerful, may be used for wet starts, permanent professional race driver engaged.

**1998**: High performance tyre barrier test specification established; pit lane should be straight 100m before pits; increased use of full light sets to supplement flag signals.

30cm in front of driver's feet (previously 15cm); frontal impact test speed increased (from 11 to 12m/s); all deformation after the test must be confined to the nose box; load in the nose push-off test increased (by 33% from 3000daN to 4000daN); survival cell side impact test introduced; obligatory automatic neutral selection when the engine stops; introduction of a stepped flat bottom; reduce front wing endplate heights (to between 5cm and 25cm above flat bottom) and length (must not extend further back than 35cm in front of the front wheel axis); no bodywork (wings) above rear wheels; rear wing max. height reduced by 10cm.

**1996:** Front wing endplates min. 10mm thick to prevent tyre damage to cars in front; data storage unit to be within survival cell; higher cockpit sides; 75mm side headrests compulsory; static load test both sides of cockpit rim; size of rear 'winglets' reduced.

**1997:** FIA Accident Data Recorder (ADR) obligatory on all cars; energy-absorbing structure on gearbox imposed, with rear impact test; energy absorption of steering wheel, column and rack must be shown by impact test; bodywork rules to exclude rear 'winglets' and midship wings; suspension must be designed to prevent contact of a front wheel with the driver's head in an accident and to provide 120° articulation of the forward lower arms, front and rear, to help retain the wheels.

**1998:** Overall width reduced from 2m to 1.8m; grooved tyres made obligatory, to reduce cornering speeds; single fuel bladder mandatory; refuelling connector must be covered; cockpit dimensions increased; side headrests extended to steering wheel; mirror size increased, 5cmx10cm to 5x12; front roll hoop test introduced; survival cell dimensions forward of dash increased; side impact test speed increased (nearly 100% more energy), site moved forward 200mm.

# In memory of . . .

**Anderson, Bob** Great Britain
Born: 19 May 1931
Died: 14 Aug 1967
Killed in a testing crash at
Silverstone.

**Ascari, Alberto** Italy
Born: 13 July 1918
Died: 26 May 1955
Killed in a testing crash at
Monza.

**Bandini, Lorenzo** Italy
Born: 21 Dec 1935
Died: 10 May 1967
Died from burns after crashing
at Monaco.

**Behra, Jean** France
Born: 16 Feb 1921
Died: 1 Aug 1959
Killed in a sports car race in
Berlin.

**Bellof, Stefan** Germany
Born: 20 Nov 1957
Died: 1 Sep 1985
Killed in a sports car race at Spa.

**Bettenhausen, Tony** United States
Born: 12 Sep 1916
Died: 12 May 1961
Died testing Paul Russo's car.

**Bianchi, Lucien** Belgium
Born: 10 Nov 1934
Died: 30 March 1969
Killed testing an Alfa Romeo at
Le Mans.

**Bonetto, Felice** Italy
Born: 9 June 1903
Died: 21 Nov 1953
Killed in the 1953 Carrera
Pan-American.

**Bonnier, Jo** Sweden
Born: 31 Jan 1930
Died: 11 Jun 1972
Killed at Le Mans.

**Bristow, Chris** Great Britain
Born: 2 Dec 1937
Died: 19 June 1960
Killed in the Belgian Grand
Prix.

**Bryan, Jimmy** United States
Born: 28 Jan 1927
Died: 19 June 1960
Died in a crash at Langhorne.

**Bueb, Ivor** Great Britain
Born: 6 June 1923
Died: 1 Aug 1959
Died after a crash in a Formula
Two race in France.

**Castellotti, Eugenio** Italy
Born: 10 Oct 1930
Died: 14 March 1957
Killed in a testing crash at
Modena.

**Cevert, François** France
Born: 25 Feb 1944
Died: 6 Oct 1973
Crashed fatally in practice for
the American Grand Prix.

**Clark, Jim** Great Britain
Born: 4 March 1936
Died: 7 April 1968
Killed in a Formula Two race at
Hockenheim.

**Collins, Peter** Great Britain
Born: 6 Nov 1931
Died: 3 Aug 1958
Killed in the German Grand
Prix.

**Courage, Piers** Great Britain
Born: 27 May 1942
Died: 21 June 1970
Died in a crash at Zandvoort.

**de Angelis, Elio** Italy
Born: 26 March 1958
Died: 15 May 1986
Killed in testing at Paul Ricard.

**de Beaufort, Carel Godin**
Holland
Born: 10 April 1934
Died: 3 Aug 1964
Killed in practice for the
German Grand Prix.

**de Portago, Alfonso** Spain
Born: 11 Oct 1928
Died: 12 May 1957
Fatal crash in the Mille Miglia
killed nine spectators and his
co-driver.

**Depailler, Patrick** France
Born: 9 Aug 1944
Died: 1 Aug 1980
Killed in testing at
Hockenheim.

**Donohue, Mark** United States
Born: 18 March 1937
Died: 19 Aug 1975
Killed in practice for the
Austrian Grand Prix.

**Fagioll, Luigi** Italy
Born: 9 June 1898
Died: 20 June 1952
Died after a practice crash at
Monaco.

**Gartner, Jo** Austria
Born: 24 Jan 1954
Died: 1 June 1986
Killed at Le Mans.

**Giunti, Ignazio** Italy
Born: 30 August 1941
Died: 10 Jan 1971
Killed in a sports car race in
Buenos Aires.

**Hansgen, Walt** United States
Born: 28 Oct 1939
Died: 7 April 1996
Fatally injured in Le Mans
trials.

**Hawkins, Paul** Australia
Born: 12 Oct 1937
Died: 26 May 1969
Died in a crash in the Tourist
Trophy.

**Hulme, Denny** New Zealand
Born: 18 June 1936
Died: 4 Oct 1992
Died of a heart attack during a
race.

**Levegh, Pierre** France
Born: 22 Dec 1905
Died: 11 June 1955
Crashed fatally at Le Mans.

**Lewis-Evans, Stuart**
Great Britain
Born: 20 April 1930
Died: 25 Oct 1958
Died from injuries in the
Moroccan GP.

**Mackay-Fraser, Herbert**
United States
Born: 23 June 1927
Died: 14 July 1957
Killed in a Formula Two race
the week after his Grand Prix
debut.

**Marimon, Onofre** Argentina
Born: 19 Dec 1923
Died: 31 July 1954
Killed in the German Grand
Prix.

**Mayer, Timmy** United States
Born: 22 Feb 1938
Died: 28 Feb 1964
Killed in practice for a race in
Tasmania.

**McLaren, Bruce** New Zealand
Born: 30 Aug 1937
Died: 2 June 1970
Killed testing at Goodwood.

**Mitter, Gerhard** Germany
Born: 30 Aug 1935
Died: 1 Aug 1969
Killed in practice for the
German Grand Prix.

**Musso, Luigi** Italy
Born: 29 July 1924
Died: 6 July 1958
Killed in the French Grand
Prix.

**Paletti, Riccardo** Italy
Born: 15 June 1958
Died: 13 June 1982
Killed in a start-line accident in
his second Grand Prix.

**Peterson, Ronnie** Sweden
Born: 14 Feb 1944
Died: 11 Sept 1978
Killed in the Italian Grand Prix.

**Pryce, Tom** Great Britain
Born: 11 June 1949
Died: 5 March 1977
Killed when a marshal ran into
his car at Kyalami.

**Ratzenberger, Roland** Austria
Born: 4 July 1962
Died: 30 April 1994
Killed in practice for the San
Marino Grand Prix.

**Revson, Peter** United States
Born: 27 Feb 1939
Died: 22 March 1974
Killed testing for the South
African Grand Prix.

**Rindt, Jochen** Austria
Born: 18 April 1942
Died: 5 Sept 1970
Fatal crash in practice at
Monza.

**Rodriguez, Pedro** Mexico
Born: 18 Jan 1940
Died: 11 July 1971
Killed in a race in Germany.

**Rodriguez, Ricardo** Mexico
Born: 14 Feb 1942
Died: 1 Nov 1962
Killed in practice for the
Mexican Grand Prix.

**Rosier, Louis** France
Born: 5 Nov 1905
Died: 29 Oct 1956
Killed in a race in Paris.

**Scarfiotti, Ludovico** Italy
Born: 18 Oct 1933
Died: 8 June 1968
Died in practice for the
Rossfeld Hill Climb.

**Schell, Harry** United States
Born: 29 June 1921
Died: 13 May 1960
Killed in practice at Silverstone.

**Schindler, Bill** United States
Born: 6 March 1909
Died: 20 Sept 1952
Killed in a race in Pennsylvania.

**Schlesser, Joe** France
Born: 18 May 1928
Died: 7 July 1968
Killed in the French Grand
Prix.

**Scott-Brown, Archie** Great
Britain
Born: 13 May 1927
Died: 19 May 1958
Killed in a race at Spa.

**Senna, Ayrton** Brazil
Born: 21 March 1960
Died: 1 May 1994
Killed in a crash in the San
Marino Grand Prix.

**Siffert, Jo** Switzerland
Born: 7 July 1936
Died: 24 Oct 1971
Killed in a non-championship
F1 race at Brands Hatch.

**Sommer, Raymond** France
Born: 31 Aug 1906
Died: 10 Sept 1950
Killed in a race in France.

**Spence, Mike** Great Britain
Born: 30 Dec 1936
Died: 7 May 1968
Killed in practice for
Indianapolis.

**Stacey, Alan** Great Britain
Born: 29 Aug 1933
Died: 19 June 1960
Killed when a bird hit him
during the Belgian Grand Prix.

**Stommelen, Rolf** Germany
Born: 11 July 1943
Died: 24 April 1983
Killed in a race at Riverside.

**Swelkert, Bob** United States
Born 20 May 1926
Died: 17 June 1956
Killed in a race in America.

**Taylor, John** Great Britain
Born: 23 March 1933
Died: 8 Sept 1966
Died of injuries sustained in the
German Grand Prix.

**Teague, Marshall** United States
Born: 22 May 1921
Died: 11 Feb 1959
Killed in a record attempt at
Daytona.

**Unser, Jerry** United States
Born: 15 Nov 1932
Died: 17 May 1959
Killed in practice at
Indianapolis.

**Villeneuve, Gilles** Canada
Born: 18 Jan 1950
Died: 8 May 1982
Killed in practice for the
Belgian Grand Prix.

**von Trips, Wolfgang** Germany
Born: 4 May 1928
Died: 10 Sept 1961
Crashed fatally at Monza,
killing 14 spectators.

**Vukovich, Bill** United States
Born: 13 Dec 1918
Died: 30 May 1955
Killed at Indianapolis.

**Wharton, Ken** Great Britain
Born: 21 March 1916
Died: 12 Jan 1957
Killed in a race in New Zealand.

**Williamson, Roger** Great Britain
Born: 2 Feb 1948
Died: 29 July 1973
Killed in the Dutch Grand Prix.

**Winklehock, Manfred** Germany
Born: 6 Oct 1951
Died: 12 Aug 1985
Killed in a race in Canada.